Street by Stre

EXETER

BUDLEIGH SALTERTON, EXMOUTH, HONITON, OTTERY ST MARY, SIDMOUTH, TOPSHAM

Broadclyst, Clyst St Mary, Cowley, Dawlish Warren, Exminster, Exton, Lympstone, Otterton, Poltimore, Starcross, Woodbury

4th edition November 2008
© Automobile Association Developments Limited 2008

Original edition printed May 2001

  This product includes map data licensed from Ordnance Survey® with the permission of the Controller of Her Majesty's Stationery Office. © Crown copyright 2008. All rights reserved. Licence number 100021153.

The copyright in all PAF is owned by Royal Mail Group plc.

 Information on fixed speed camera locations provided by RoadPilot © 2008
RoadPilot® Driving Technology.

All rights reserved. No part of this publication may be reproduced, stored in a retrieval system, or transmitted in any form or by any means – electronic, mechanical, photocopying, recording or otherwise – unless the permission of the publisher has been given beforehand.

Published by AA Publishing (a trading name of Automobile Association Developments Limited, whose registered office is Fanum House, Basing View, Basingstoke, Hampshire RG21 4EA. Registered number 1878835).

Produced by the Mapping Services Department of The Automobile Association. (A03813)

A CIP Catalogue record for this book is available from the British Library.

Printed by Oriental Press in Dubai

The contents of this atlas are believed to be correct at the time of the latest revision. However, the publishers cannot be held responsible or liable for any loss or damage occasioned to any person acting or refraining from action as a result of any use or reliance on any material in this atlas, nor for any errors, omissions or changes in such material. This does not affect your statutory rights. The publishers would welcome information to correct any errors or omissions and to keep this atlas up to date. Please write to Publishing, The Automobile Association, Fanum House (FH12), Basing View, Basingstoke, Hampshire, RG21 4EA. E-mail: streetbystreet@theaa.com

Ref: ML109x

Key to map pages	ii–iii
Key to map symbols	iv–1
Enlarged map pages	2–3
Main map pages	4–63
Index - towns & villages	64
Index - streets	65–73
Index - featured places	73–74
Acknowledgements	74

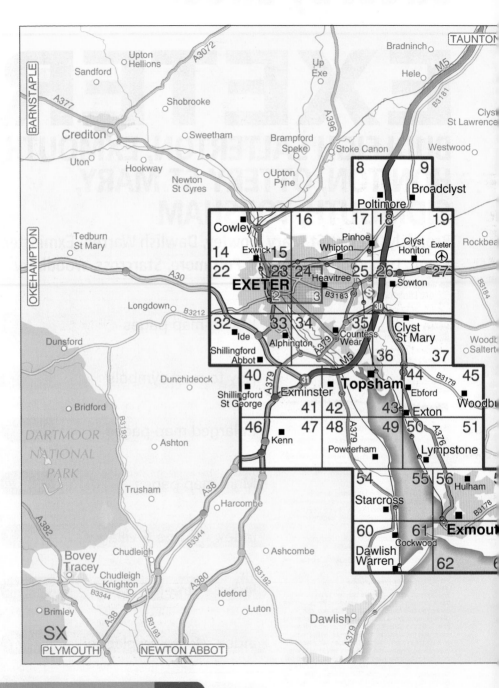

The map contains the following labels:

TAUNTON
BARNSTAPLE
OKEHAMPTON
Bradninch
Upton Hellions
Sandford
Up Exe
Hele
Westwood
Clyst St Lawrence
Shobrooke
A3072
A377
A396
M5
B3181
Crediton
Sweetham
Brampford Speke
Stoke Canon
Uton
Hookway
Upton Pyne
8
9
Broadclyst
Poltimore
Newton St Cyres
Cowley
16
17
18
19
Tedburn St Mary
Exwick
15
Pinhoe
Whipton
Clyst Honiton
Exeter
Rockbea
14
22
23
24
25
26
27
EXETER
Heavitree
2
3
B3183
Sowton
B3184
Longdown
B3212
A30
32
33
34
35
Clyst St Mary
Woodb
Salter
Ide
Alphington
Countess Wear
Dunsford
Shillingford Abbot
A379
M5
36
37
Dunchideock
40
44
45
Exminster
Topsham
Ebford
Woodbu
Bridford
Shillingford St George
41
42
43
Exton
DARTMOOR NATIONAL PARK
B3193
A38
A382
46
47
48
49
50
51
Ashton
Kenn
Powderham
Lympstone
Trusham
54
55
56
Harcombe
Starcross
Hulham
B3178
Chudleigh
60
61
Exmout
Bovey Tracey
Cockwood
Chudleigh Knighton
Dawlish Warren
62
Brimley
B3344
A380
Ideford
Luton
Dawlish
A379
B3192
B3193
Ashcombe
SX
PLYMOUTH
NEWTON ABBOT

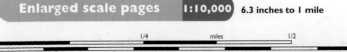

Enlarged scale pages   1:10,000   6.3 inches to 1 mile

0   1/4   miles   1/2
0   1/4   1/2   kilometres   3/4   1

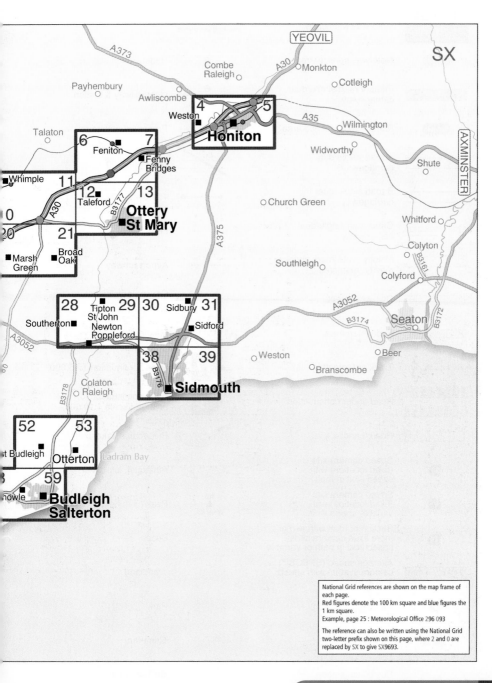

National Grid references are shown on the map frame of each page.
Red figures denote the 100 km square and blue figures the 1 km square.
Example, page 25 : Meteorological Office 296 093

The reference can also be written using the National Grid two-letter prefix shown on this page, where 2 and 0 are replaced by SX to give SX9693.

4.2 inches to 1 mile **Scale of main map pages** 1:15,000

Junction 9	Motorway & junction	Railway & minor railway station	
Services	Motorway service area	Underground station	
	Primary road single/dual carriageway	Light railway & station	
Services	Primary road service area	Preserved private railway	
	A road single/dual carriageway	*LC* Level crossing	
	B road single/dual carriageway	Tramway	
	Other road single/dual carriageway	Ferry route	
	Minor/private road, access may be restricted	Airport runway	
← ←	One-way street	County, administrative boundary	
	Pedestrian area	Mounds	
	Track or footpath	**17** Page continuation 1:15,000	
	Road under construction	**3** Page continuation to enlarged scale 1:10,000	
	Road tunnel	River/canal, lake, pier	
30	Speed camera site (fixed location) with speed limit in mph	Aqueduct, lock, weir	
V	Speed camera site (fixed location) with variable speed limit	465 ▲ Winter Hill Peak (with height in metres)	
40	Section of road with two or more fixed camera sites; speed limit in mph or variable	Beach	
50⟶ ⟵50	Average speed (SPECS™) camera system with speed limit in mph	Woodland	
P	Parking	Park	
P🚌	Park & Ride	Cemetery	
🚌	Bus/coach station	Built-up area	
	Railway & main railway station		

	Industrial/business building			Abbey, cathedral or priory
	Leisure building			Castle
	Retail building			Historic house or building
	Other building	Wakehurst Place NT		National Trust property
	City wall			Museum or art gallery
A&E	Hospital with 24-hour A&E department			Roman antiquity
PO	Post Office			Ancient site, battlefield or monument
	Public library			Industrial interest
i	Tourist Information Centre			Garden
i	Seasonal Tourist Information Centre			Garden Centre Garden Centre Association Member
	Petrol station, 24 hour Major suppliers only			Garden Centre Wyevale Garden Centre
†	Church/chapel			Arboretum
	Public toilet, with facilities for the less able			Farm or animal centre
PH	Public house AA recommended			Zoological or wildlife collection
	Restaurant AA inspected			Bird collection
Madeira Hotel	Hotel AA inspected			Nature reserve
	Theatre or performing arts centre			Aquarium
	Cinema			Visitor or heritage centre
	Golf course			Country park
▲	Camping AA inspected			Cave
	Caravan site AA inspected			Windmill
	Camping & caravan site AA inspected			Distillery, brewery or vineyard
	Theme park		•	Other place of interest

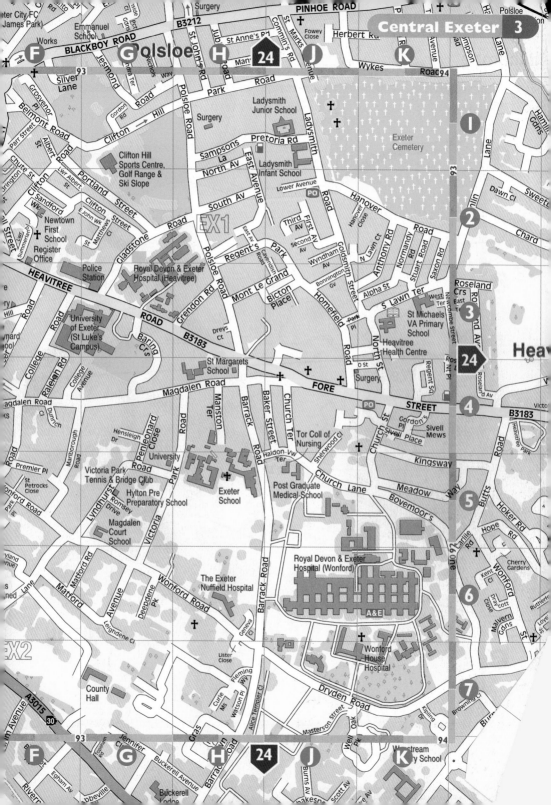

A B C D

3 08   09

1 00

Talewater

Feniton

Sherwood
Farm

Lincoln Cl
EN   Mo
Ackland Pk   High
                      Feniton
Station   Road CE Primary
✝   Sch
LC   York Wells
Feniton   Crs
Station   AV
The Signals
The Burland
Exeter York Crs

2

Roman Road

99

3

River Tale

4

Escot
Park

◀ **11**

0 98

❋ Escot

5

A30

3 08   09

Dig
Wood   A30

A   angland   **B**   ▼ **12**   **C**   **D**

Lane   Gosford

Gosford

ston
m

I grid square represents 500 metres

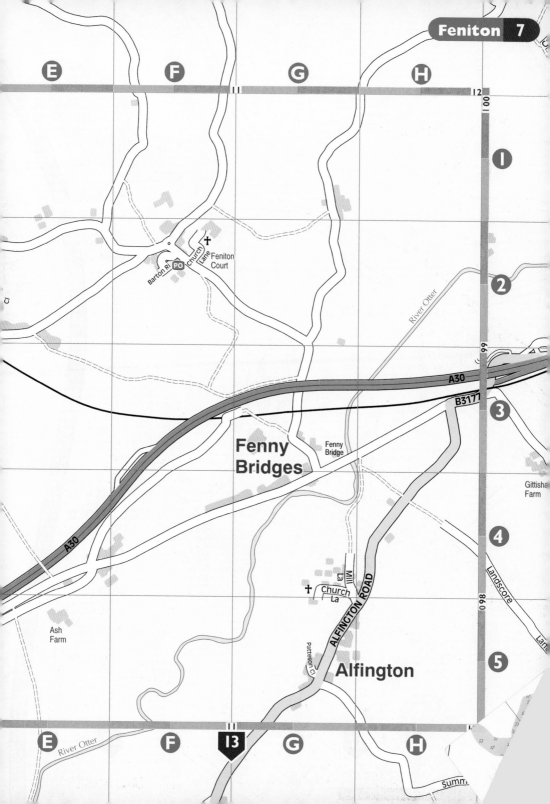

E F G H I

River Otter

A30

B3177

Barton Rl PO Church Lane
Feniton Court

Fenny Bridges

Fenny Bridge

Gittisha Farm

Landscore Lane

Mill La
Church La

ALFINGTON ROAD

Alfington

Patteson Cl

Ash Farm

A30

River Otter

Summ

8

Cutton

A **296** B Belfield House C **97** D

Danes

1

98

2

Ratsloe

97

3

Moor Lane

M5

Hatchland Road

4

† **Poltimore**

Dandy Lane

5

Home Farm

Poltimore House

096

A **296** B C **97** D

A **17** B C **18** D

1 grid square represents 500 metres

Park

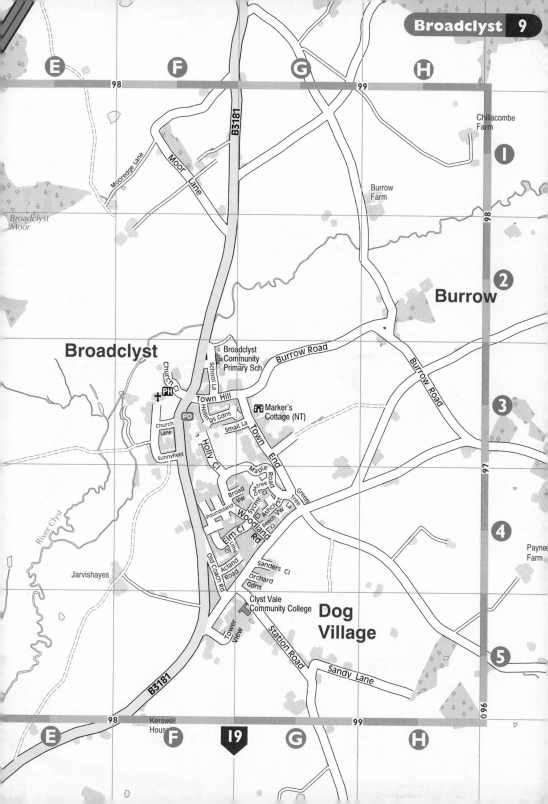

E **F** **G** **H**

98
99

Chillacombe
Farm

I

98

Mooredge Lane

Moor Lane

B3181

Burrow
Farm

*Broadclyst
Moor*

2

Burrow

97

Broadclyst

Church Cl

PH

✝

Broadclyst
Community
Primary Sch

School La

Burrow Road

Burrow Road

3

Town Hill

PO

Church
Lane

Hellings Gdns

Town Hill

Marker's
Cottage (NT)

Small La

Sunnyfield

Holly Cl

Town End Rd

4

River Clyst

Maple Cl

Oak Tree Cl

Sycamore

Broad
Vw

Ashclyst

Beech Vw

Tree Green

Poundsland

Woodland Rd

Elm Cl

Lime Cl

Payne
Farm

Jarvishayes

Old Coach Rd

Acland Road

Sanders Cl

Orchard
Gdns

Clyst Vale
Community College

**Dog
Village**

5

Tower View

Station Road

Sandy Lane

96

B3181

Kerswell
House

98
99

E **F** **G** **H**

19

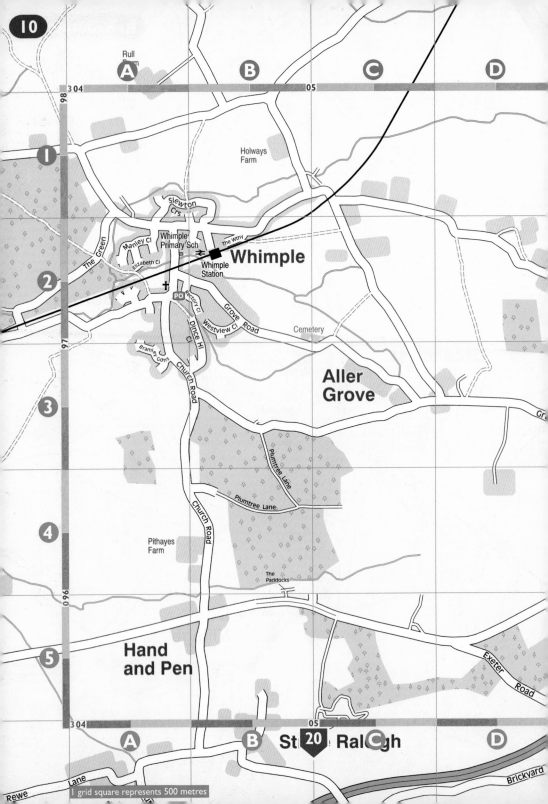

A **B** **C** **D**

3 04 05

98

1

Rull Farm

Holways Farm

Slewton Crs

Whimple Primary Sch

Manley Cl

Elizabeth Cl

The Wthy

Whimple

Whimple Station

2

97

The Green

PO

Rectory Cl

Westview Cl

Dince Hl Cl

Grove Road

Cemetery

Bramley Gdns

Church Road

Aller Grove

3

Plumtree Lane

Plumtree Lane

Gr

4

96

Pithayes Farm

Church Road

The Paddocks

Exeter Road

5

Hand and Pen

3 04 05

A **B** **St** **20** **Ral** **gh** **D**

Rewe Lane

Brickyard

1 grid square represents 500 metres

New Barn
Farm

E   F   G   H

07   08

Talaton
Farm

Escot
Park

✳ Escot

Larkbeare

Larkbeare
Court

1

6

Larkbeare

2

Avenue

97

A30

3

Birdcage

4

Lane

Cadhay
Wood

96

12

5

Straitgate
Farm

Birdcage

Lane

E   F   G   H

07   08

B ER ROA
21
B3174

A30

Pitfield
Farm

EXETER ROA

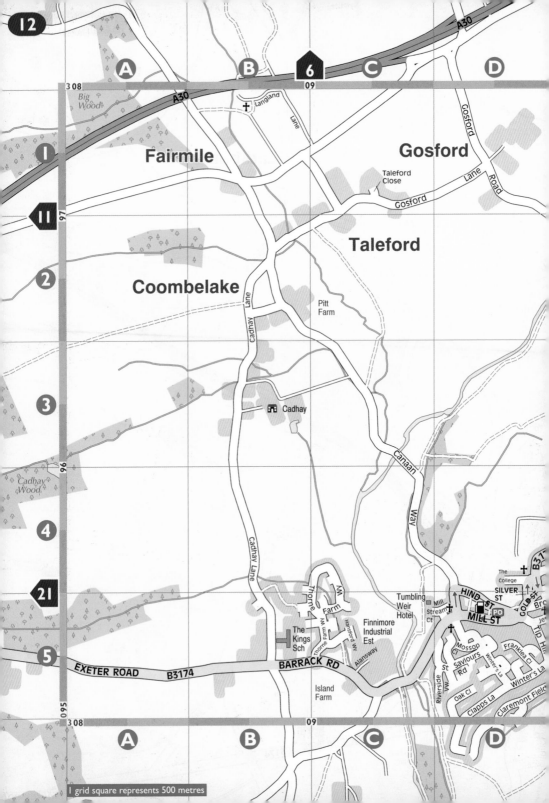

Farm

Alfington

E F **7** G H

Patteson Cl

River Otter

Summer Lane

Pitham Lane

Gosford Road

Woodford

Four Elms Farm

ALFINGTON ROAD

Holcombe Lane

Holcombe

B3177

BUTTS HILL

Meadow Cl

Butts Road

Washbrook Vw

St Ann Cl

Katherines La

Hgr Ridgeway

OTTERY ST MARY

Ridgeway

New Lane

Kennaway Rd

Coleridge Rd

St Sarans

Raleigh Road

Snts Md

New St Beauvale Cl

Patteson Dr

Kings Av

Furzebrook

Ch La

Hills Cl

P of F Cl

BRKdl

Chineway Road

Sandhill St

Street

Yonder St

Spring Gdns

Hgr Spring

Grandisson Dr

Slade Cl

Slade Cl

Great Well Farm

Yonder V

Orchard Cl

St Budeaux Cl

Chineway Gdns

Chineway Gdns

Homefield

Lane

Chineway Gdns

Longdogs

ngdogs

Ottery St Mary Primary Sch

St Marys Park

Knightstone La

Slade Road

Slade Road

Slade Farm

Gerw..

E F G H

Rill Farm

I

2

3

4

5

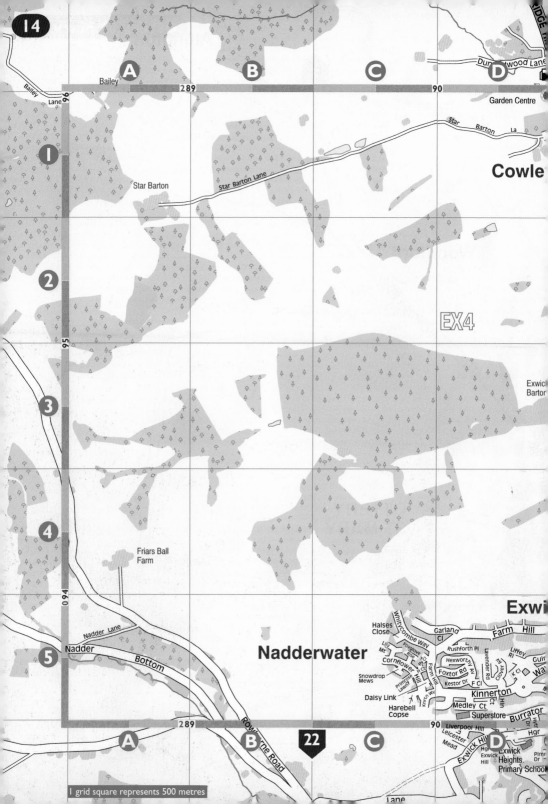

14

A Bailey   B   C   D

Bailey Lane

2 89   90

Dunwood Lane

Garden Centre

96

1

Star Barton Lane

Star Barton

Star Barton La

Cowle

95

2

EX4

3

Exwick Barton

4

Friars Ball Farm

094

Nadder Lane

5 Nadder

Bottom

Exwi

Halses Close

Whitycombe Way

Garland Cl

Farm Hill

Nadderwater

Rushforth Pl

Liffey Rd

Lily Mt

Foxglove

Rose

Cornflower

Hexworthy Av

Lavender Rd

Primrose Lawn

Farm Hill

Foxtor Rd

Snowdrop Mews

Kestor Dr

F Cl

Clover

Guir Wa

Kinnerton

Daisy Link

Knett Wy

Medley Ct

Harebell Copse

Superstore

Burrator

A   2 89   Rowhorne Road   B   **22**   C   90   D

Liverpool Hill

Leicester Mead

Exwick Hill

Exwick Heights Primary School

Lane

1 grid square represents 500 metres

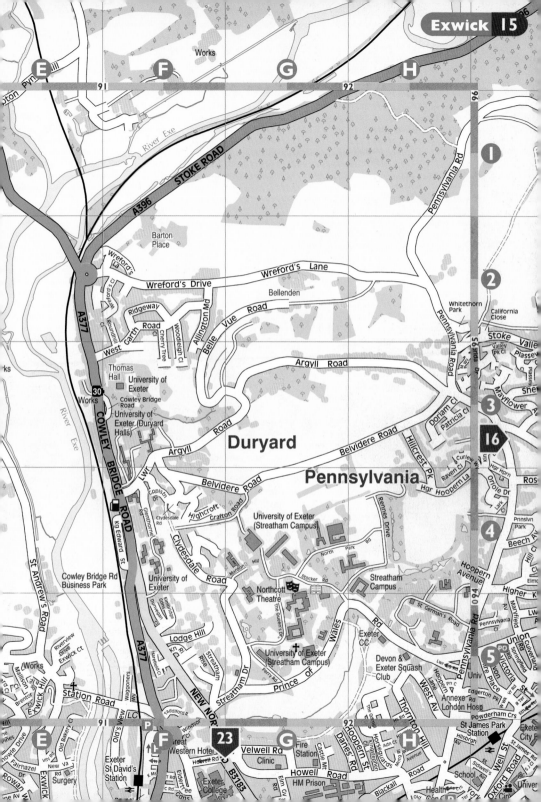

Works

E   F   G   H

91   92   96

River Exe

STOKE ROAD

A396

I

Barton
Place

Wreford's La

Wreford's Drive   Wreford's Lane   **2**

Bellenden

Ridgeway   Belle Vue Road   Whitethorn
Park   California
Close

West Garth   Road   Cherry Tree   Woodleigh Cl   Allington Rd   Pennsylvania Rd   Stoke   Valle
Valley   Plassey
Pk Cl   She

A377   Thomas
Hall   University of
Exeter   Argyll   Road   Mayflower   **3**

Works   30   Cowley Bridge
Road   Doran Ct   Patricia Cl   **16**

University of
Exeter (Duryard
Halls)   **Duryard**   Belvidere Road   Hillcrest Pk   Curlew Cl   Hgr Hprn   Oriole Dr   Ros

River Exe   Argyll   Road   **Pennsylvania**   Raven Cl   Hgr Hooper La

LWr   Belvidere   Road   Rennes Drive   North   **4**
Coppish Dr   Highcroft   Grafton Road   University of Exeter   Park   Rd   Pnnsln
Park   Beech Cl

Clydesdale
Rd   (Streatham Campus)   North   Hooper   Elmc
Avenue   Higher K

St Andrew's Road   Cowley Bridge Rd
Business Park   University of
Exeter   Clydesdale   Road   Maldon   Hill   Stocker   Rd   Streatham
Campus   St German's Road   Maryfield   LWr

Lodge Hill   Northcott
Theatre   The Queen's Dr   Exeter
CC   Pennsylvania   Union   PO   **5**
Riverview
Drive
Exwick Ct   University of Exeter
(Streatham Campus)   Devon &
Exeter Squash
Club   Lwr Ld Rd   Edgerton Pk   Victoria   Place   Univ

Works   Lodge Hill   Prince   of   Wales   Rd   London Hosp   Annexe Rd   Powderham Crs

Exwick Hill   Station Road   NEW NOR   Streatham Dr   Thornton Hill   West Av   St James Park
Station   Exete
City

91   P   E   F   **23**   G   Fire
Station   Velwell Rd   H   Hilsbrgh

Exeter
St David's
Station   Great
Western Hotel   Velwell Rd
Clinic   Castle Mt   Howell   Road   School   St Sidwell's   Well St   Oxford Road

Exwick
Surgery   Exeter
College   B3183   HM Prison   Blackall   Health Ce   York

Polsloe

EXETER

18 Farm

A 297 **8** **B** **C** 98 **D** B3181

Kerswell House

I

Park Farm

2 95 Parkside Crs **30** Parkside Road B3181 PINN HILL

West Clyst

Mosshayne Lane

Mosshayne

Pinn Court Farm

Pinncourt Lane

LANE BINDON ROAD Vicarage La Broadparks Janesway **3** Saxon Avenue **17** PO MAIN ROAD Honiton La Parkers La **Pinhoe** Sunnymoor Cl Cross La Ross Cl Pinn Va Road Orchard Harrington Gdns Sedgeclaire Close Langaton La Oak Close B3181 Causey Gdns Peamoor Dr Langaton Cl Ashi Farm Cl Oakler **4** Station Causey La Langaton Fairview Ter

hoe Surgery LC Rews Mdw Rews Pk Drive stps Cl Grasslands Dr Babblebrook Mews Monkerton Dr Farmhouse Av Pinn La Old Pinn La Min La

5 Rd

Best Western Gipsy Hill Country House Hotel Gipsy Hill La

Titchbarn Lane Titchbarn Lane Langaton Lane Mill La Mosshayne Lane

Blackhorse Lane **Blackhorse**

Surgery Honiton

Junction 29 **A** 297 **B** Redhayes **26** **C** 98 **D** Endsleigh Crescent Honiton Road **40** HONITON

Ellen Tinkham Special School Pinn Lane

An Ar

I grid square represents 500 metres

village

Station Road

Sandy Lane

E

9

F

G

H

99

3 00

96

I

Elbury Farm

ckhill

Wishford
Farm

Young
Hayes Farm

2

Lodge
Trading
Estate

Blue
Hayes

Hungry Fox
Est

Station Road

Bluehayes Lane

Parsons

95

3

Clyst Av

Cotterell Rd

Shortcott Cl

Treasbeare Lane

Works

4

Hayes
Farm

Works

Waterslade Lane

0 94

5

Works

Ship La

St Michael's
Hill
St Michael's

Exeter Airport

Church Road

**Clyst
Honiton**

E

Clyst
Honiton
School

F

27

G

3 00

Exeter
Airport

Exeter Airport
Industrial
Estate

H

Fair Oak
Cl

Exeter Airport
Business Park

Business
Park

Oak Rd

4D A30

B3184

B3184

Hand
and Pen

A   **B**   **10**   **C**   **D**

3 04   05

Strete Raleigh

Rewe   Lane   Turkey   Lane   Brickyard

1

95

Strete
Farm

A30   Brickyard Road

2

Turkey   Lane   Allercombe   Hill   Tele

Allercombe

Allercombe   Lane   New   Rd

3

94

Marsh Green Lane   Palmer's Lane

**Marsh
Green**

4

Lane

Great
Houndbeare
Farm

Little
Houndbeare
Farm

5

0 93

Mile   Lane   Houndbeare   Lane   Oak   Rd   Oak
Rd

Quarter   Lane

3 04   05

A   **B**   **C**   **D**   B7

I grid square represents 500 metres

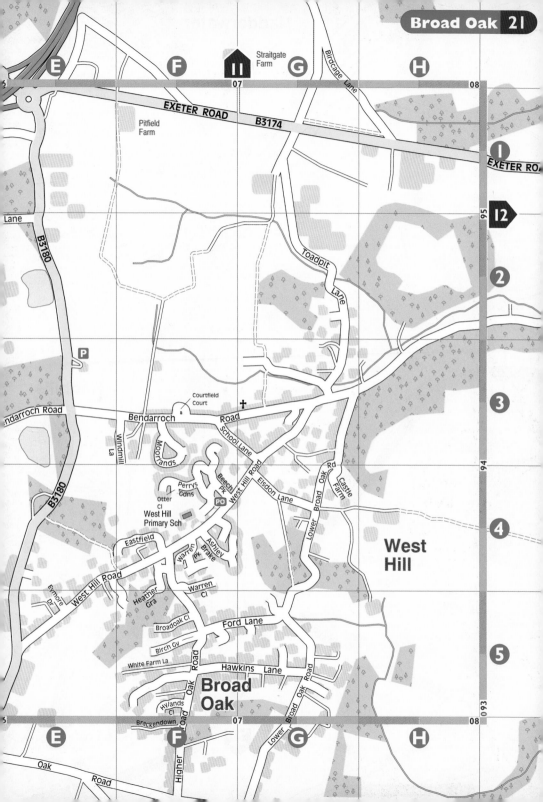

E F **11** Straitgate Farm G H

I EXETER ROAD

12

2

3

4

5

EXETER ROAD B3174

Pitfield Farm

Birdcage Lane

Toadpit Lane

Lane

B3180

P

Bendarroch Road

Courtfield Court

Bendarroch Road

School Lane

Windmill La

Moorlands

Perrys Gdns

Beech Pk

Otter Cl

West Hill Primary Sch

PO

West Hill Road

Elsdon Lane

Oak Rd

Lower Broad Oak

Castle Farm

West Hill

B3180

Eastfield

West Hill Road

Eymore Dr

Heather Gra

Warren Pk

Ashley Brake

Warren Cl

Broadoak Cl

Birch Gv

White Farm La

Hawkins Lane

Ford Lane

Road

Higher

Broad Oak Road

Lower

Broad Oak

Hylands Cl

Brackendown

Oak Road

E F G H

08

07

08

07

95

94

93

Nadderwater

22

Nadder

Nadder Bottom

A

289

B

14

C

Rowhorne Road

Close
ombe Way
Cl
Rushforth Pl
Liffey
Cl
Guinn
Way
Mt
Foxglove
Cornflower
Hexwort
Lavender Rd
Clover
Snowdrop Mews
Princess Lawn
Foxtor Rd
Farm Hill
Kestor Dr
F Cl
Medley Ct.
Kinn
on
Link
Harebell Copse

90

Superstore
Burrator D

I

93

Exwick

Lane

Liverpool Hill
Leicester
Mead
Exwick Hill
Hgr
Exwick Hill
Exwick Heights Primary School
Pimrst
Dr
Hgr

Redhills

St Peters Mt

Canterbury Rd
Peterborough Road
Chester Cl
Cheltenham
Winc

Gloucester

Road

Guildford C
Edinburgh
Lincoln Rd

Chelmsford Road
Lichfield Rd
F.C
Westminster Rd

2

Osbornes Farm

Redhills

Hadrian Drive

Addison Cl
Antonine Crs
Redhills

30

Tedburn Road

92

Eastwood

Nadder Brook

Barley Lane

Redhills
Mount
Barley

Redhills

3

TEDBURN ROAD A30

Barley Lane

Islewo
Mdw
Prescot Road
Charnley Av
High
Wellswood Gdns
B'combe
Green Lane

Nadder Park Road

4

Westwood Lane

Tedburn Road

The Quaries

Barley Farm Rd
Barley Farm Rd
Berkshire Dr
M

Black Hat Lane

Webby's Farm

Barley Lane Special School

Croft Cha
Essex
West
Cl
Heron
Way
Swallow
Dove Wy
Sampher Cr
Dunsford Garden
Sussex Cl
Wiltshire Cl
Dorset Av
Hampshire
Somerset Av
BOW
Wentwort

5

BAKERS HILL

Pocombe Bridge

POCOMBE HILL

Perridge Cl

B3212

Vuefield
Hambeer
Lane
Browl

LONGDOWN ROAD

091

289

A30

A

ege Lane

Scratch

Lane

B

32

C

90

Little John's Cross H

D

12

es Lane

k's
m

PH

1 grid square represents 500 metres

Waterslade Lane

Works

Ship La

St Michael's Hill

Clyst Honiton School

Clyst Honiton

St Michael's Ct

Church Side

Exeter Airport

E **F** **19** **G** **H** 300

Exeter Airport

Exeter Airport Industrial Estate

Exeter Airport Business Park

Fair Oak Cl

Business Park

I

B3184

B3184

Fair Oak Rd

OAD A30

A30

93

Bishop's Ct Lane

Marlborough Farm

ymond's arm

Wroford Manor

2

3

Holbrook Farm

92

Sp Fa

Denbow Farm

4

Axehayes Farm Caravan Site

Hill Barton Business Park

Mushroom Rd

5

160

Woodlands Way

Meadow Cl

Valley Rd

Wood

Glen Close

Hazelmead Rd

H Rd

99

E **F** **37** Blackmore 300 **G** **H**

Hill Barton Business Park

Blackmore

Blackmore Rd

A3052

Hill Barton Business Park

A30

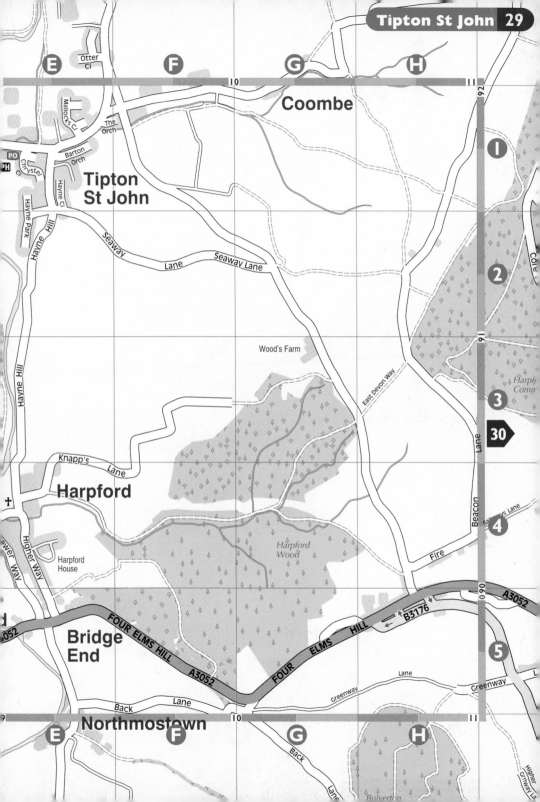

E   Otter Cl   F   G   H

Mallocks C

10

Coombe

The Orch

PO

Chrystel

PH

Barton Orch

I

Hayne Park

Hayne Hill

Tipton St John

Seaway Lane

Seaway Lane

Seaway Lane

92

91

2

Wood's Farm

East Devon Way

Harpfo Comm

Hayne Hill

3

30

Knapp's Lane

Beacon Lane

Harpford

Saways Lane

4

Harpford Wood

Fire

Higher Way

Harpford House

ower Way

Harpford Wood

90

A3052

B3176

Bridge End

FOUR ELMS HILL

FOUR ELMS HILL

A3052

5

A3052

Greenway

Lane

Greenway

Back   Lane

10

Northmostown

Back

11

E   F   G   H

Bulverton

Higher Grnway La

Cotford

Sidbury

Sidford

Castle Hill House

Ebdon Farm

Buckley Farm

Buckton Farm

Knowle House

Map labels:

Roncombe
Cotford Side
Orchard Side
Davids
Ridgeway Cl
Ridgeway
COTFORD ROAD
Sidbury CE Primary Sch
Church St
Hatway Hill
East Devon Way
Greenhead
FORE ST
Bridge St
Buckley Road
CHAPEL STREET
A375
Buckley Road
Northground Lane
Ottery Lane
Buckton Lane
Under Lane
River Sid
TWO BRIDGES RD
Brook Cl
Wr Brook Mdw
Lwr Brook Mdw
Brook Meadow
Brook La
Frys La
SCHOOL ST
Sid V Cl
Castle Hl Vw
Englands
Hamilton Cl
PO
South Lawn
Orchard Av
Drake's Avenue
Warrens
Byres Lane
Parkhorse Cl
CHURCH STREET
Harcombe Lane
Harcombe Flds
Harcombe
Lane East
Steven's Crs Cl
Fleming Av
Byres Cl
Jubilee Gdns
TROW HILL
Malden Road
Breside Rd
Hides Rd
HIGH ST A3052
Fortes Road
A3052
Trow Hill
Trow Hall
Vineycroft Lane
Sidmouth College
Grimley Mdw
Lwr Griggs

39

14 15

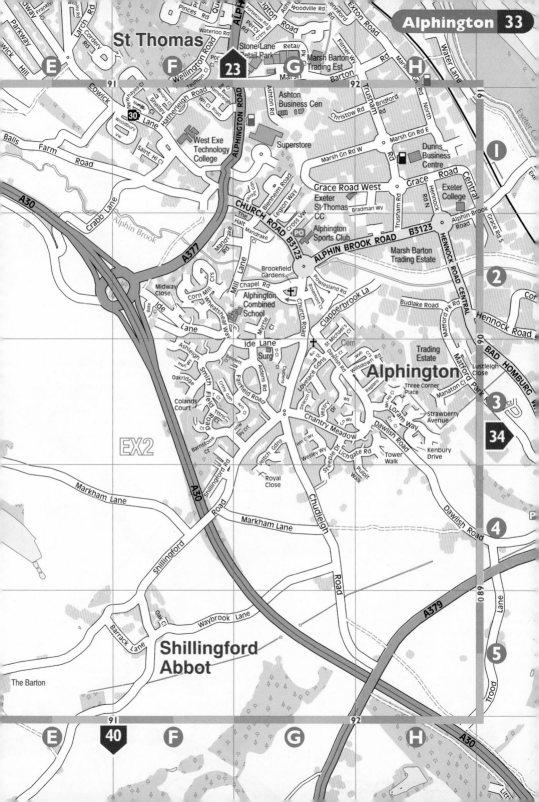

E

F

G

H

25

E

F

42

G

H

I

2

3

36

4

5

Ludwell Lane

Russell Wy

Clyst Heath

Grange

RYDON

A379

A379

95

Superstore

Russell Wy

Russell Way

Old Rydon Cl

M5

M5

91

Sandy Park

Pynes Hill

Countess Wear

West of England School & College

Garden Centre

Old Rydon Lane

Old Rydon Ley

Old Rydon Lane

Kestrel Business Park

Clyst Works

Clyst Road

90

Newcourt Barton

A379 RYDON LANE

Golf Course

Works

Surgery

Exeter Golf & Country Club

Topsham Road

Lwr Wear Rd

PO

Works

Whitehall La

Countess Wear Combined School

Lakeside Avenue

Wear Barton Road

Newport Road

Hgr Wear Rd

Wear Cl

Seabrook Av

Towerfield

Highfield

089

Lower Wear

Works

The Copse

First Av

Second Av

Third Av

Exeter Road

M5

Newcourt Road

Exeter Canal

River Exe

Topsham RFC

Topsham Town AFC

Denver Road

Wessex Close

The Retreat Dr

Gordon Rd

Riverside Rd

Hamilton Rd

Retreat Road

High Street

Ferry Road

Station Road

95

96

TOPSHAM

The Topsham School

Fire Stn

Milbury

Axehayes Farm
Caravan Site

E F

27

G

Hill Barton
Business Park

H

Woodlands Way

Hazelmead
Rd

Rosewood

Meado
Cl

Glen
H Rd

Close

99 ley Rd

Blackmore Rd

Hill Barton
Business Park

Blackmore
Rd

3 00

Mushro Rd

1 6

A3052

A3052

I

Crealy
Barton

Greendale
Lane

Crealy
Adventure
Park

90

orks

Shepherds
Farm

2

Little Bridge
Business Park

3

Kenniford
Farm

Greendale Lane

Lower Road

4

Heathfield
Farm

Higher

0 89

lyst St

eorge

Bushayes
Farm

5

Sch

Postlake
Farm

Lower
Pilehaves
Farm

B3179

3 00

E

99

44

F

G

H

WOODBURY ROAD

Steven's Crs Cl

Avenue
Fleming
Jubilee Gdns
Malden Road
B'esi
Hides Rd
Road

E

F

Fortescue Road

31
14

Trow Hall

G

A3052
Trow Hill

H
15

Vineycroft Lane

Sidmouth College

Primley Md
Primley Rd
Primley Gdns
Road

Lwr Griggs

Grigg's Lane

Higher Fortescue

I

Salcombe Caravan

Livonia Rd

River Sid

Sid Road

Sidcliffe

Sid
Milltown La

Questant La
d La
sdara Rd
Green Mt
Clevedon Pk

Glenrise Way
Regency Gate

Brownlands Road
Brownlands Cl

Mdw Vw C

dwood Road

Salcombe Hill Road

Alma Lane

ombe lose
Kestell Rd
Southway Road

Laskeys Lane

Road

Salcombe Regis

Dunscombe

✝

Wynyard Farm

2

Coombe Wood Farm

3

088

4

087

5

E
14

F

G

15

H

3

P

Topsham Town AFC
Cemetery
Gordon Rd
Hamilton Rd
side Rd
Denver Road
Sunhill Av
Pound La
High Street
Ashford Road
Orch Wy
Retreat Road
Elm Grove Rd

E   **F**   **36**   **G**   **H**

97   98

House

Chapel H

M

The Topsham School
Grove Hill
Topsham Station
Grove Hill
Balmoral Gdns
Greatwood Ter
LC
Elm Cv Av

EX3

Innkeeper's Lodge

76

I   **Eb**

EXMOUTH ROAD

Ferry Road
Station Road
Follett Rd
Fire Stn
Parkfield Road
Undermill Ter
PH
Bridge Hill

Marsh Barton
Darts Farm

Topsham Sailing Club
Surgery
Exe St
PO
Victoria Road
Globefield
Surgery

88

Old Edford La
The Ridings

2

Fore Street
White St
Holman Way
Altamira
Min Av
Globe Lane
Monmouth St
Bowling Gn Road

The Globe Htl
PH
Works
Monmouth Hl
Hgr Shapter St
Nth St
Lower Shapter St
Hope House Montessori School

A376

3

Strand
Topsham Museum
MVW
Lower Strand
Treslian Gdns
Shapter St
Mount Howe

River Clyst

44

Station Road
South West Coast Path
Exeter Canal

Riversmeet House

87

Green Lane

4   **Exton**

Front
River
PH
Avocet Dr
Sandpiper Drive
Nurseries Close
Exton

Exton Station
Station Rd

5

Turf

E   **F**   **49**   **G**   **H**

97   98
980

South West C

South West Co

Lympstone Command

44

A **B** **C** **D**

298

37
99

I

Innkeeper's
Lodge

Marsh
Ba...

arts Farm

Ebford

WOODBURY ROAD

B3179

Chapel Hill

Woodbury Rd

Lady
Seawards
CE Prim Sch

Bushayes
Farm

Postlake
Farm

Ebford Lane

The Ridings

Lower Lane

Old Ebford La

2

88

Higher Bagmores
Farm

3

43

87

A376

EXMOUTH ROAD

Lower Bagmores
Farm

Rydon Farm

4

Green Lane

River

Exton

Avocet Dr

Sandpiper
Drive

Exton Lane

Nurseries
Close

Barton Cl

Btn
Mk

Mill Lane

Rydon Lane

PH

Exton
Station

Station Rd

Station Road

The Avenue

5

086

298

Lane

A **B** **C** **D**

50
99

Porter's

Lympstone

†

Stony Lane

A37...

1 grid square represents 500 metres

Business Park

Sayes Lea

Lane

White Cross

E

Lower Pilehaves Farm

F

Bond's Lane

G

Village

Browns Farm Caravan Park

H

Road

Toby Lane

I

Bond's Lane

Water La

Lane

Farm

88

WOODBURY ROAD

B3179

2

Pound Lane

Cottles Lane

Cemetery

Parsonage Way

Summerfield

P C

Long Park

Stokes Mead

Lane

Oakhayes

Road

Longmeadow

Gvts

Woodbury Castle

Broadmead

Bn La

CE Primary School

Webbers Farm Caravan & Camping Park

3

Cl V Cl

Bv

Orchard Close

GLOBE HILL

Mirey La

Flower St

Woodbury

87

The Arch

Jarent Cl

Fulford Way

Town Lane

Furze Road

Critchards

Works

PO

Surg.

Park Cl

Beeches Cl

BROADWAY

Park Way

Ford Farm

4

B3179

Rydon Lane

Venmore Farm

5

086

00

E

F

01

51

G

Woodmanto

H

Stony

Lane

E F 41 G H

93 94
86

Old Dawlish Road

I

enn

† Belle vue

River Kenn Works

Old Dawlish Road

2

85

Pennycombe Farm

3

48 ▶ orthy F

Whitcombe

4

84

5

gher
hornton Farm

Haydon Common

E F 93 G H 94

Ash Farm

E   Turf

F

43
97

G

H

98
86

I   Lympstone Commando Station

River Exe

2

85

3

50

Powderham †

Church Road

4

084

Starcross Yacht Club

5

Powderham Castle

97

98

E

54

F

G

H

Penhayes Rd

South West Coast Path

rcombe Lane

N HILL

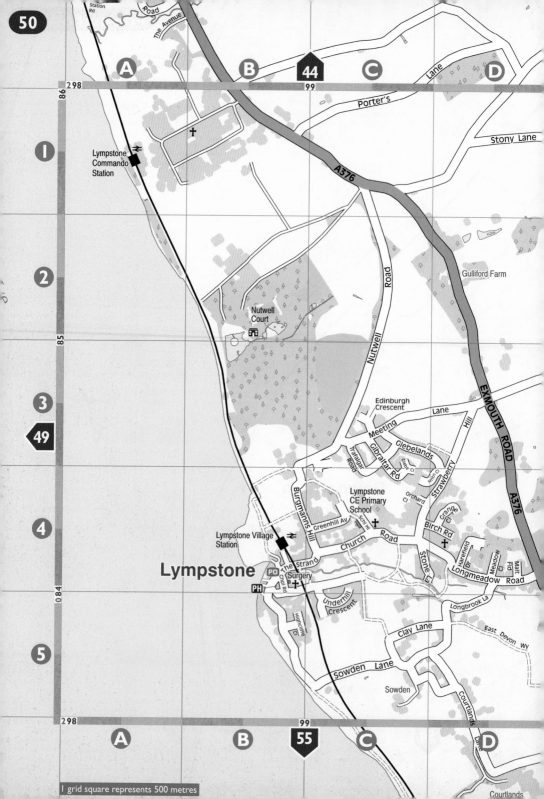

A   B   C   D

P

1

Yettington

shlers orch

Sawmill Lane

Yettington Road

2

Hayes Barton
(Home of Sir Walter Raleigh)

Hayes Lane

Priory Cl

Church La
All Saints
Cl

Vicarage Road

Pynes Cl
Cranes La
Wynards Cl

Wynards Rd

Tref Lisis

High Street

Middletown Lane

Russell Dr

East
Budleigh

3

Hayes
Wood

Hayeswood La

Drakes
Prim
Sch

Oak

Orchard
Cl

Brookfield Road

Middle Street

Lower Budleigh

BUDLEIGH

4

Shortwood Common

Tidwell Lane

EX9

5

alditch

A   B   C   D

Pooh Cottage
Holiday Park

Tidwell
House

59

Kersbrook

E F G H

College
Agriculture

River

North
Star

Little Chocker
Chocker

I

Mausoleum &
Remains
of Church

B3178

Ottery Street

Ladram Road

Obelisk

Sleap Hill

Otterton
Primary
Sch

Watering
Ct

Dukes
Ct

Bell Street

2

Fore Street

Otterton Mill

Church Hill

Maunder's H

Roper's Lane

Isaac
Ct

Orchard Dr

Lea Rd

Behind

Hayes

Vieux Cl

Otterton

Piscombe Lane

EAST BUDLEIGH ROAD

Frogmore Road

Jacketts

Park La

85

3

Syon
House

Stantyway Road

4

Pulhayes
Farm

84

Otterton
Park

5

E F G H

Warren

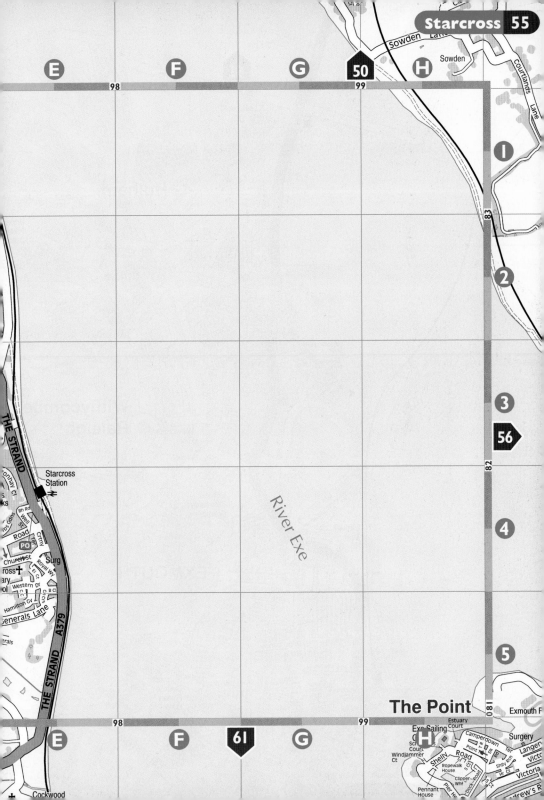

Sowden Lane

Courtlands Lane

Sowden

E 98 F G 50 99 H

I 83

2

3

56

82

4

River Exe

Starcross
Station

Starcross
Station

THE STRAND

Bh Rd
Well St
Crm
Cnhay Ct
ks

Road

PO

Church St
Surg
ross
ary
ol
Western Dr
Hamilton Gv
Generals Lane
A379
THE STRAND A379

erals

5

The Point

181

Exmouth F

Estuary
Court

Exe Sailing
Point

Camperdown

Surgery

Langer

Sch
Court
Windjammer
Ct

Shelly

Shelly Road

Shelly Rd

Victe

Ropewalk
House

Clipper
House

Pennant
House

Victoria

drew's R

E 98 F 61 G 99 H

Cockwood

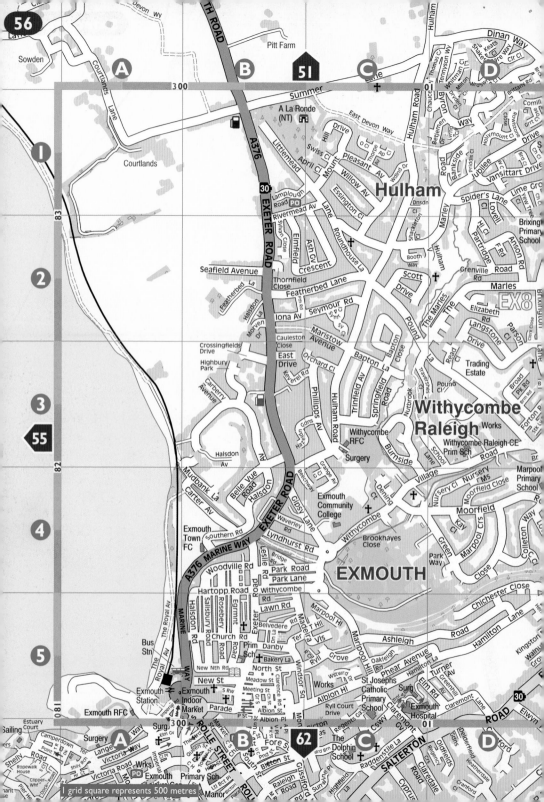

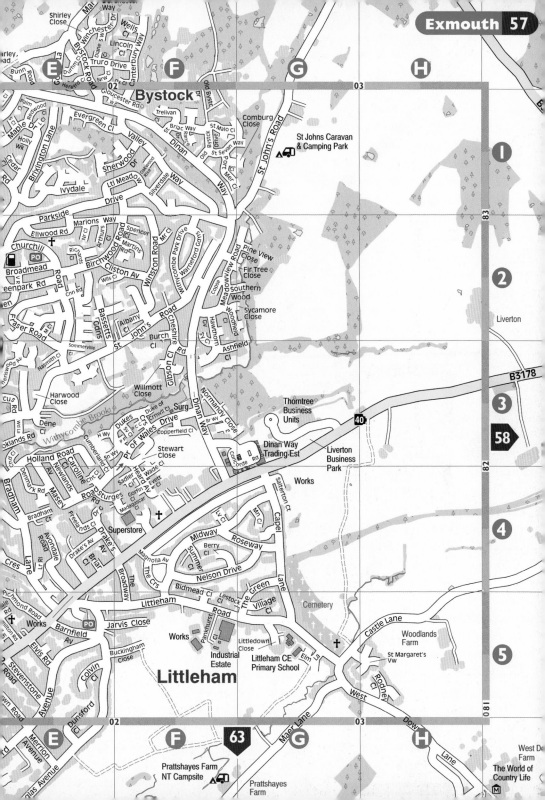

E F G H

Bystock

Shirley Close
Wells Cl
Lincoln Cl
Truro Drive
Winchester Cl
Canterbury Way
Gloucester Rd
Trelivan
Briac Way
Comburg Close

St Johns Caravan
& Camping Park

I

Maple Dr
Redwood
Holly Wk
Cedar
Brixington Lane
Ivydale
Evergreen Cl
Valley
Sherwood Dr
Silverdale Way
Dinan Way
St Malo Cl
St Port Mer Cl
St Sevan Way
Old Bystock Dr

St John's Road

2

Liverton

Parkside
Ellwood Rd
Marions Way
Spencer Cl
Arthurs
Martins
Richards
Birchwood Road
Cliston Av
Winston Road
Withycombe Park Drive
Wareford Road
Pine View Close
Fir Tree Close
Southern Wood
Sycamore Close
Woodfield
Meadowview Road

B3178

Churchill
PO
Broadmead
Greenpark Rd
Bassetts Gdns
Albany
St John's Road
Cheshire Rd
Gibson Cl
Burch Cl
Hawthorn
Ashfield Cl

3

58

Fraser Road
Sommerville
Nasmith Cl
Harwood Close
Dene Cl
Willmott Close
Normandy Close
Dinan Way
Thorntree Business Units

40

Oaklands Rd
Holland Road
Caroline
Newlands
Masey
Denmark Rd
Bradham
Freelands Dr
Cumberland Cl
Dukes
Pr of Wales Drive
Copperfield Cl
Stewart Close
Dinan Way Trading Est
Liverton Business Park

Works

4

Bradham Lane
Avondale Road
Drake's Av
Briar Cl
Sadler
Sturges Road
Gorfin
Wade Cl
Madagascar Cl
Superstore
Midway
Roseway
Sumner
Berry
Magnolia Av
Nelson Drive
Capel Lane
Sutterton Ct

Works

Richmond Road
Barnfield Av
PO
Jarvis Close
Buckingham Close
Colvin Cl
The Broadway
The Crs
Bidmead Cl
Lestock Cl
The Green
Village Cl
Littleham Road
Cemetery

Castle Lane
Woodlands Farm

5

Stevenstone Road
Elvis Rd
Dunsford Cl
Works
Panhurst
Industrial Estate
Littledown Close
Littleham CE Primary School
Elm
St Margaret's Vw
Rodney Cl

Littleham

West

E F 63 G H

Merrion Avenue
Prattshayes Farm NT Campsite
Maer Lane
Prattshayes Farm
Dow
Lane
West De Farm

The World of Country Life

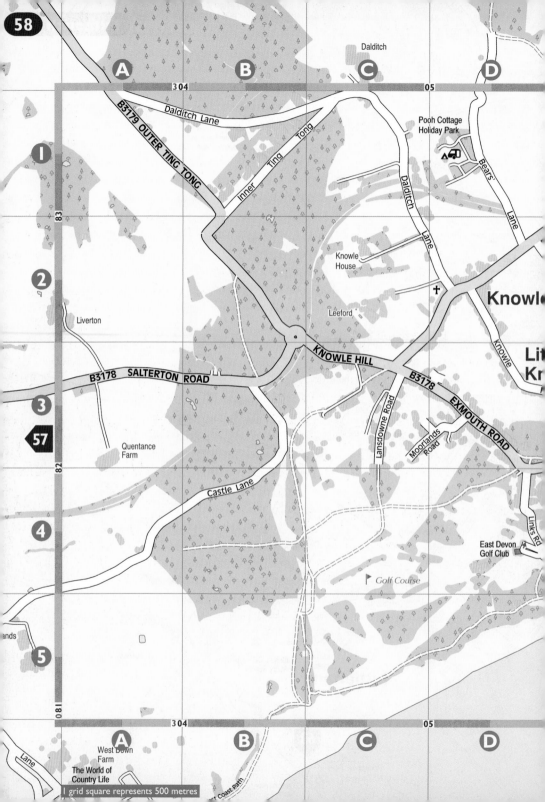

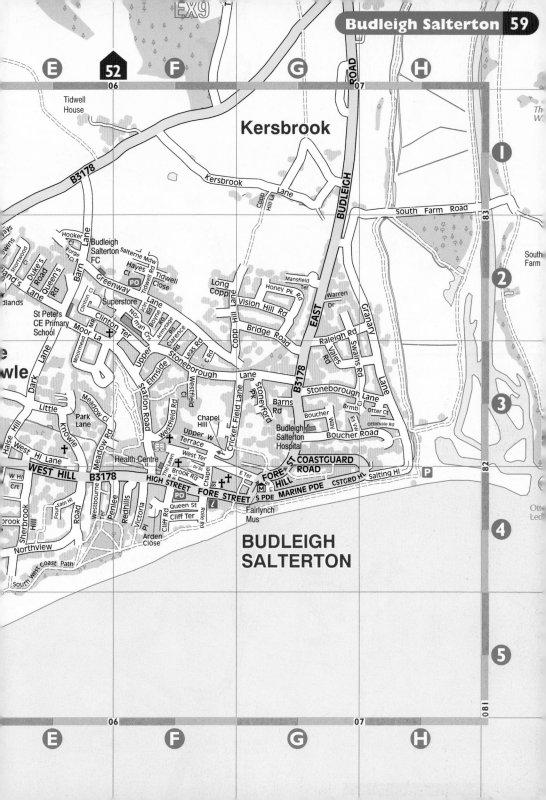

E 52 F G ROAD H

Kersbrook

Tidwell House

B3178

Kersbrook Lane

Copp Hill Lane

South Farm Road

BUDLEIGH

South Farm

I

Hooker Cl
Forge Cl
Budleigh Salterton FC
Salterne Mdw
Hayes Cl
Tidwell Close
PO
Tidwell Rd
Greenway

Long Copp

Mansfield Ter
Honey Pk Rd
Warren Dr

83

2

South Farm

Dukes Road
Queen's Rd
Shortwood
Barn Lane
Lane
Clinton Cl
John Ter
Norman Crs
Boyne Rd
Clarence Rd
Armytage Rd
C Rd
Vision Hill Rd
EAST

Superstore
St Peters CE Primary School
Moor La
Clinton Ter
Upper Stoneborough
Leas Rd
Copp Hill Lane
Bridge Road
Raleigh Rd
Vales Rd
Swains Rd
Granary Lane

B3178
Greenway

2

3

Dark Lane
Elmside
Westfield Cl
Lane
Stoneyford Pk
Stoneborough Lane
Brmb
Otter Ct
ottervale Rd
Moormead
Meadow Cl
Meadow Rd
Station Road
Westfield Rd
Cricket Field Lane
Stoneyford Rd
Boucher Way
Es Vw
Boucher

Little Knowle
Park Lane
West Hl Lane
Chapel Hill
Barns Rd
Budleigh Salterton Hospital
Boucher Road

3

Halse Hill
West Hl Crt
W Hl Crt
Health Centre
The Lawn
Upper W Terrace
West Ter
Pr Pl
Chapel
E Ter
FORE ST
HILL
COASTGUARD ROAD
P

WEST HILL
B3178
HIGH STREET
PO
Brook Rd
FORE STREET
M
S PDE
MARINE PDE
CSTGRD HL
Salting Hl

Sherbrook Hill
Northview
Westbourne Ter
Penlee
Redhills
Fountain Hl
Road
Victoria Pl
Queen St
Cliff Rd
Cliff Ter
Rolle Rd
Chapel St
Arden Close
Fairlynch Mus

4

South West Coast Path

BUDLEIGH SALTERTON

82

Otter Led

4

180

5

E 06 F G 07 H

60

A ⟨296⟩ B **54** C 97 D

81

①

Cofford Farm

EXETER ROAD

Church Road

Southbro

Cofton Lane

Westwood Hill

Middlewood

②

Cofton Country Holidays

Westwood

Cofton Hill

80

Cofto

E

③

Orchard

Port Road

Exeter Rd

79

Branscombe Lane

④

EXETER ROAD A379

Shutterton Farm

Dawlish Warren

Langdon Hospital

Shutterton Lane

Sherwell Cl

⑤

Windsor Dr

Hazelwood

W. W.

Lakeside

Bracken

Terwy

Millcroft arm

Poplar

Skylark

Cedar

Beechwoo

40

Shutterton Bridge

Sandpiper

A ⟨296⟩ B

Lady's Mile Holiday Park

C

97 Golden Sands Holiday Park

D

Week Lane

Langdon Farm

Littleweek La

Week Road

Mo

I grid square represents 500 metres

THE STRAND

E **F** **55** **G** **H**

The Point

98 99

Exmouth RFC

Exe Sailing
Club

Estuary
Court

Camperdown

Surgery

Schooners
Court

Langerwell

I

Windjammer
Ct

Shelly

Ropewalk
House

Point

Road

Victoria

Victoria Ra

Clipper

Wharf

Pennant
House

Pier Head

Dock

St Andrew's Rd

2

Mamhead
View

Cavendish E

Hotel

80

Cockwood
Primary
School

School Hill

Rd

Cockwood

Kenbury
Crescent

Dawlish Warren Road

3

62

tdon

Eastdon
House

Dawlish
Warren

Dawlish Warren
National Nature
Reserve

4

079

Golf Course

Warren Golf
Club

5

Dawlish
Warren
Station

Surgery

P

East Devon Way

Peppermint
Park

Pine
Tree

Beach Road

98 99

E **F** **G** **H**

Pleasant

Coast Path

Elvis Rd
Av
Works
Pa
Littledown
Close
St Margar
Vw
Woodlands
Farm

Stevenstone

Colvin Cl

Buckingham
Close

Littleham CE
Primary School

West
Down
Lane

Rodney
Cl

West Dow
Farm

The World of
ry Life

Littleham

Industrial
Estate

Elm

Dunsford
Cl

Merrion
Avenue

57

Maer Lane

E

F

G

H

I

02

03

18

Prattshayes Farm
NT Campsite

Prattshayes
Farm

Meadow
Crescent

Devon Cliffs
Holiday Park

Douglas Avenue

Works

2

Gore Lane

Maer
Farm

Gore Lane

Gore Lane

80

Lane

Gore Lane

3

Hill
Foxholes

South West Coast Path

High Land
of Orcombe

South West Coast Path

Maer Local
Nature Reserve

Sandy
Bay

Straight
Point

4

079

5

E

F

G

H

02

03

E

F

G

H

Alfington 7 G5	Duryard 15 G3	Littleham 57 F5	Sid 39 E2
Allercombe 20 A3	East Budleigh 52 C3	Little Knowle 58 D3	Sidbury 31 F1
Aller Grove 10 C3	Eastdon 60 D3	Littletown 5 E4	Sidford 31 E4
Alphington 33 H3	Ebford 44 A1	Lower Wear 35 E4	Sidmouth 38 D5
Blackhorse 18 C5	Exeter 2 A5	Lympstone 50 A4	Southerton 28 B3
Bridge End 29 E5	Exminster 42 A3	Markham Cross 32 C4	South Town 54 C2
Broadclyst 9 E3	Exmouth 56 C4	Marley Hayes 51 H4	Sowton 26 B2
Broad Oak 21 F5	Exton 44 A4	Marsh Green 20 A4	Starcross 54 D4
Budleigh Salterton 59 G4	Exwick 14 D5	Monkerton 17 H5	Stoke Hill 16 C3
Bulverton 38 B1	Fairmile 12 A1	Nadderwater 14 B5	Stowford 30 A5
Burrow 28 B5	Feniton 6 D1	Newton Poppleford 28 D5	Strete Raleigh 20 B1
Burrow 9 H2	Fenny Bridges 7 G3	North Star 53 H1	Taleford 12 C2
Bystock 57 F1	Gosford 12 C1	Otterton 53 G2	Talewater 6 A1
Clyst Honiton 19 F5	Hamlet 4 A4	Ottery St Mary 13 F4	Tipton St John 29 E1
Clyst St George 36 D4	Hand & Pen 10 A5	Pennsylvania 15 G4	Topsham 42 D1
Clyst St Mary 26 C5	Harpford 29 E4	Pinhoe 18 A3	Venn Ottery 28 B2
Cockwood 61 E1	Heavitree 24 D2	The Point 55 H5	Weston 4 A3
Cofton 60 D2	Honiton 4 C5	Poltimore 8 C4	Westwood 60 C2
Coombe 29 C1	Hulham 56 C1	Powderham 49 F4	Whimple 10 B2
Coombelake 12 A2	Ide 32 C2	Ratsloe 8 A2	Whipton 17 F5
Cotmaton 38 B4	Kenn 47 E1	Redhills 22 D3	Withycombe Raleigh 56 C3
Countess Wear 35 E1	Kennford 40 D5	St Thomas 23 F5	Woodbury 45 G3
Cowley 14 D1	Kenton 54 A1	Salcombe Regis 39 H1	Woodford 13 E2
Crealy Barton 37 H1	Kersbrook 59 G1	Sandy Gate 26 A4	Woodmanton 51 G1
Dawlish Warren 60 D4	Knowle 58 D2	Shillingford Abbot 33 F5	Yettington 52 A1
Dog Village 9 C5	Larkbeare 11 G1	Shillingford St George 40 B2	

USING THE STREET INDEX

Street names are listed alphabetically. Each street name is followed by its postal town or area locality, the Postcode District, the page number, and the reference to the square in which the name is found.

Standard index entries are shown as follows:

Abbeville CI *EXS* EX2 ....**24** B5

Street names and selected addresses not shown on the map due to scale restrictions are shown in the index with an asterisk:

Acland Ter *EXN* EX4 * **2** E1

GENERAL ABBREVIATIONS

ACC	ACCESS	DR	DRIVE	INT	INTERCHANGE	PREC	PRECINCT
ALY	ALLEY	DRO	DROVE	IS	ISLAND	PREP	PREPARATORY
AP	APPROACH	DRY	DRIVEWAY	JCT	JUNCTION	PRIM	PRIMARY
AR	ARCADE	DWGS	DWELLINGS	JTY	JETTY	PROM	PROMENADE
ASS	ASSOCIATION	E	EAST	KG	KING	PRS	PRINCESS
AV	AVENUE	EMB	EMBANKMENT	KNL	KNOLL	PRT	PORT
BCH	BEACH	EMBY	EMBASSY	L	LAKE	PT	POINT
BLDS	BUILDINGS	ESP	ESPLANADE	LA	LANE	PTH	PATH
BND	BEND	EST	ESTATE	LDG	LODGE	PZ	PIAZZA
BNK	BANK	EX	EXCHANGE	LGT	LIGHT	QD	QUADRANT
BR	BRIDGE	EXPY	EXPRESSWAY	LK	LOCK	QU	QUEEN
BRK	BROOK	EXT	EXTENSION	LKS	LAKES	QY	QUAY
BTM	BOTTOM	F/O	FLYOVER	LNDG	LANDING	R	RIVER
BUS	BUSINESS	FC	FOOTBALL CLUB	LTL	LITTLE	RBT	ROUNDABOUT
BVD	BOULEVARD	FK	FORK	LWR	LOWER	RD	ROAD
BY	BYPASS	FLD	FIELD	MAG	MAGISTRATES'	RDG	RIDGE
CATH	CATHEDRAL	FLDS	FIELDS	MAN	MANSIONS	REP	REPUBLIC
CEM	CEMETERY	FLS	FALLS	MD	MEAD	RES	RESERVOIR
CEN	CENTRE	FM	FARM	MDW	MEADOWS	RFC	RUGBY FOOTBALL CLUB
CFT	CROFT	FT	FORT	MEM	MEMORIAL	RI	RISE
CH	CHURCH	FTS	FLATS	MI	MILL	RP	RAMP
CHA	CHASE	FWY	FREEWAY	MKT	MARKET	RW	ROW
CHYD	CHURCHYARD	FY	FERRY	MKTS	MARKETS	S	SOUTH
CIR	CIRCLE	GA	GATE	ML	MALL	SCH	SCHOOL
CIRC	CIRCUS	GAL	GALLERY	MNR	MANOR	SE	SOUTH EAST
CL	CLOSE	GDN	GARDEN	MS	MEWS	SER	SERVICE AREA
CLFS	CLIFFS	GDNS	GARDENS	MSN	MISSION	SH	SHORE
CMP	CAMP	GLD	GLADE	MT	MOUNT	SHOP	SHOPPING
CNR	CORNER	GLN	GLEN	MTN	MOUNTAIN	SKWY	SKYWAY
CO	COUNTY	GN	GREEN	MTS	MOUNTAINS	SMT	SUMMIT
COLL	COLLEGE	GND	GROUND	MUS	MUSEUM	SOC	SOCIETY
COM	COMMON	GRA	GRANGE	MWY	MOTORWAY	SP	SPUR
COMM	COMMISSION	GRG	GARAGE	N	NORTH	SPR	SPRING
CON	CONVENT	GT	GREAT	NE	NORTH EAST	SQ	SQUARE
COT	COTTAGE	GTWY	GATEWAY	NW	NORTH WEST	ST	STREET
COTS	COTTAGES	GV	GROVE	O/P	OVERPASS	STN	STATION
CP	CAPE	HGR	HIGHER	OFF	OFFICE	STR	STREAM
CPS	COPSE	HL	HILL	ORCH	ORCHARD	STRD	STRAND
CR	CREEK	HLS	HILLS	OV	OVAL	SW	SOUTH WEST
CREM	CREMATORIUM	HO	HOUSE	PAL	PALACE	TDG	TRADING
CRS	CRESCENT	HOL	HOLLOW	PAS	PASSAGE	TER	TERRACE
CSWY	CAUSEWAY	HOSP	HOSPITAL	PAV	PAVILION	THWY	THROUGHWAY
CT	COURT	HRB	HARBOUR	PDE	PARADE	TNL	TUNNEL
CTRL	CENTRAL	HTH	HEATH	PH	PUBLIC HOUSE	TOLL	TOLLWAY
CTS	COURTS	HTS	HEIGHTS	PK	PARK	TPK	TURNPIKE
CTYD	COURTYARD	HVN	HAVEN	PKWY	PARKWAY	TR	TRACK
CUTT	CUTTINGS	HWY	HIGHWAY	PL	PLACE	TRL	TRAIL
CV	COVE	IMP	IMPERIAL	PLN	PLAIN	TWR	TOWER
CYN	CANYON	IN	INLET	PLNS	PLAINS	U/P	UNDERPASS
DEPT	DEPARTMENT	IND EST	INDUSTRIAL ESTATE	PLZ	PLAZA	UNI	UNIVERSITY
DL	DALE	INF	INFIRMARY	POL	POLICE STATION	UPR	UPPER
DM	DAM	INFO	INFORMATION	PR	PRINCE	V	VALE

VA....VALLEY
VIAD....VIADUCT
VIL....VILLA
VIS....VISTA
VLG....VILLAGE
VLS....VILLAS
VW....VIEW
W....WEST
WD....WOOD
WHF....WHARF
WK....WALK
WKS....WALKS
WLS....WELLS
WY....WAY
YD....YARD
YHA....YOUTH HOSTEL

POSTCODE TOWNS AND AREA ABBREVIATIONS

BUD....Budleigh Salterton
DAW....Dawlish
EX....Exeter
EXM....Exmouth
EXN....Exeter north
EXS....Exeter south
HON....Honiton
OTT....Ottery St Mary
REXNE....Rural Exeter north & east
REXSW....Rural Exeter south & west
SID....Sidmouth
TOP/EXT....Topsham/Exton

Index - streets

A

Abbeville Cl *EXS* EX2....24 B5
Abbey Ct *EXS* EX2....26 A3
Abbey Rd *EXN* EX4....16 C5
Abbot's Rd *EXN* EX4....16 B5
Ackland Pk *HON* EX14....6 D1
Acland Rd *EXN* EX4....2 E1
REXNE EX5....9 F4
Acland Ter *EXN* EX4 *....2 E1
The Acorns *EXN* EX4 *....16 A3
Addington Ct *EXN* EX4....23 H1
Addison Cl *EXN* EX4....22 D2
Alansway *OTT* EX11....12 C5
Albany Cl *EXM* EX8....57 F2
Albany Rd *EXN* EX4....23 F4
Alberta Crs *EXN* EX4....16 C4
Albert Pl *EXM* EX8....62 B1
Albert St *EX* EX1....3 F1
Albion Hl *EXM* EX8....56 C5
Albion Pl *EXM* EX8....62 B1
EXN EX4....24 A1
Albion St *EXM* EX8....56 B5
EXN EX4....23 F3
Aldens Rd *EXS* EX2....33 G3
Alderson Dr *EX* EX1....25 G3
Aldrin Rd *EXN* EX4....16 A3
Alexandra Ter *EXM* EX8....62 A1
EXN EX4....24 B1
Alexandria Rd *SID* EX10....38 C2
Alfington Rd *OTT* EX11....13 F2
Alford Cl *EX* EX1....25 F1
Alford Crs *EX* EX1....25 E1
Alfranza Cl *EX* EX1 *....25 E2
Alice Templer Cl *EXS* EX2....3 H7
Allercombe Hl *REXNE* EX5....20 C2
Allercombe La *REXNE* EX5....20 B3
Allervale Cl *EXS* EX2....25 E4
Allhallows Ct *EXN* EX4....2 A4
Allington Md *EXN* EX4....15 F3
All Saints Cl *BUD* EX9....52 C3
All Saint's Rd *SID* EX10....38 C4
Alma La *SID* EX10....39 E4
Alpha St *EX* EX1....3 K3
Alphin Brook Rd *EXS* EX2....33 G2
Alphington Rd *EXS* EX2....33 G1
Alphington St *EXN* EX4....2 A5
Alston Ter *EXM* EX8....62 A1
Altamira *TOP/EXT* EX3....43 F1
Ambassador Dr *EX* EX1....25 H1
Amyatt's Ter *SID* EX10....38 C5
Andrew Cl *SID* EX10....30 B5
Anne Cl *EXN* EX4....16 B4
Anson Rd *EXM* EX8....56 D2
Anthony Rd *EX* EX1....3 K3
Antonine Crs *EXN* EX4....22 D2
Apple Cl *EXM* EX8....56 C1
Apple Farm Gra *EXS* EX2....25 H5
Apple La *EXS* EX2....25 H5
April Cl *EXM* EX8....56 B1
The Arcade *EXN* EX4 *....2 C2
Archibald Rd *EX* EX1....2 E3
The Arch *REXNE* EX5....45 F3
Arcot Gdns *SID* EX10....38 D2
Arcot Pk *SID* EX10....38 D2
Arcot Rd *SID* EX10....38 D2
Arden Cl *BUD* EX9....59 F4
Arena Pk *EXN* EX4....17 E4
Argus Cl *HON* EX14....5 F2
Argyll Ms *EXN* EX4 *....15 F4
Argyll Rd *EXN* EX4....15 G3
Armstrong Av *EXN* EX4....16 A3
Armytage Rd *BUD* EX9....59 F2
Arthurs Cl *EXM* EX8....57 E2
Arundel Cl *EXS* EX2....33 G3
Ascerton Cl *SID* EX10....38 D3
Ascerton Rd *SID* EX10....38 D3
Ashclyst Vw *REXNE* EX5....9 G4
Ash Farm Cl *EX* EX1....18 A4
Ashfield Cl *EXM* EX8....57 F3
Ashford Rd *TOP/EXT* EX3....43 E1
Ash Gv *EXM* EX8....56 C2
Ashleigh *EXS* EX2....33 F3
Ashleigh Cl *EXN* EX4....23 E2
Ashleigh Mount Rd *EXN* EX4....23 E3
Ashleigh Rd *EXM* EX8....56 C5
HON EX14....4 D2
Ashley Brake *OTT* EX11....21 F4
Ashley Crs *SID* EX10....38 C1
Ashton Rd *EXS* EX2....23 G5
Ashwood Rd *EXS* EX2....23 G5
Aspen Cl *EXS* EX2....25 F4
HON EX14....4 B4
Athelstan Rd *EX* EX1....2 E3
Atkinson Cl *EXN* EX4....16 D5
Attwyll Av *EXS* EX2....24 D3
Austen Cl *EXN* EX4....17 F5
Avalon Cl *EXN* EX4....16 D3
Avenue Mezidon Canon
HON EX14....5 F3
The Avenue *TOP/EXT* EX3....44 A5
Avocet Dr *TOP/EXT* EX3....44 A4
Avocet Rd *EXS* EX2....26 A2
Avondale Rd *EXM* EX8....57 E4
EXS EX2....24 D3
Axminster Rd *HON* EX14....5 H3

B

Babblebrook Ms *EX* EX1....18 A5
Back La *SID* EX10....28 C5
Badger Cl *EXS* EX2....25 G3
HON EX14....5 F1
Bad Homburg Wy *EXS* EX2....34 A4
Badon Cl *EXN* EX4....16 D3
Bagshot Av *EXS* EX2....24 A5
Bailey St *EXN* EX4....2 C2
Baker Cl *SID* EX10....30 C5
Bakers Hl *EXS* EX2....22 B5
Baker St *EXS* EX2....3 H4
Bakery La *EXM* EX8....56 B5
Balfour Cl *HON* EX14....5 F3
Balfour Gdns *SID* EX10....38 C2
Balfours *SID* EX10....38 C2
Balls Farm Rd *EXS* EX2....33 E1
Balmoral Gdns *TOP/EXT* EX3....43 E1
Bampfylde La *EXN* EX4....2 D3
Bampfylde St *EX* EX1....2 D2
Banfield Wy *HON* EX14....4 D4
Bankside *EXM* EX8....56 D1
Bapton Cl *EXM* EX8....56 C3
Bapton La *EXM* EX8....56 C3
Barbican Steps *EXN* EX4....2 A4
Baring Crs *EX* EX1....3 G3
Baring Ter *EXS* EX2....2 D7
Barle Cl *EXS* EX2....25 G4
Barley Farm Rd *EXN* EX4....22 D4
Barley La *EXN* EX4....22 C3
Barley Mt *EXN* EX4....22 D3
Barnardo Rd *EXS* EX2....2 D6
Barnes Cl *HON* EX14....4 D4
Barnfield Av *EXM* EX8....57 E5
Barnfield Crs *EX* EX1 *....2 D3
Barnfield Hl *EX* EX1....2 E3
Barnfield Rd *EX* EX1....2 D3
Barn Hayes *SID* EX10....38 B1
Barn La *BUD* EX9....59 E2
Barns Rd *BUD* EX9....59 G3
Barnstone Ct *EXS* EX2....33 F3
Barrack La *EXS* EX2....33 E5
Barrack Rd *EXS* EX2....3 H6
OTT EX11....12 B5
Barrowdale Cl *EXM* EX8....51 G5
Bartholomew St East
EXN EX4....2 A3
Bartholomew St West
EXN EX4....2 A4
Bartholomew Ter *EXN* EX4 *....2 A4
Barton Cl *TOP/EXT* EX3....44 A4
Barton La *EXS* EX2....32 D5
Barton Ms *TOP/EXT* EX3....44 A5
Barton Orch *SID* EX10....29 E1
Barton Ri *HON* EX14....7 F2
Barton Rd *EXS* EX2....23 E5
Bassetts Gdns *EXM* EX8....57 E2
Bate Cl *EXS* EX2....33 F2
Bath Cl *HON* EX14....6 D2
Bathern Rd *EXS* EX2....25 G4
Bath Rd *EXM* EX8....62 B2
Battishorne Wy *HON* EX14....4 D4
Baxter Cl *EXS* EX2....25 G5
Bay Trees *REXSW* EX6....46 C1
Bazley Sq *EX* EX1....17 H5
Beach Rd *DAW* EX7....61 E5
Beacon Av *EXN* EX4....16 C5
Beacon Heath *EXN* EX4....17 E4
Beacon Hl *EXM* EX8....62 B1
Beacon La *EXN* EX4....16 D5
Beacon Pl *EXM* EX8....62 B1
The Beacon *EXM* EX8....62 B1
Bears' La *BUD* EX9....58 D1
Bear St *EX* EX1....2 C4
Beatlands Rd *SID* EX10....38 D4
Beaufort Rd *EXS* EX2....23 F4
Beauvale Cl *OTT* EX11....13 E4
Beaworthy Cl *EXS* EX2....33 F1
Bedford Sq *SID* EX10....38 D5
Bedford St *EXN* EX4....2 C2
Bedland's La *BUD* EX9....58 D2
Beech Av *EXN* EX4....16 A4
Beech Cl *HON* EX14....4 C5
REXNE EX5....9 G4
Beeches Cl *REXNE* EX5....45 F4
Beech Pk *OTT* EX11....21 F4
Beechway *EXM* EX8....56 B4
Beechwood Crs *DAW* EX7....60 D5
Beggars La *HON* EX14....4 C3
Behind Hayes *BUD* EX9....53 G2
Belgrave Rd *EX* EX1....2 E2
Belle Isle Dr *EXS* EX2....2 E7
Belle Vue Cl *REXSW* EX6....47 E2
Belle Vue Rd *EXM* EX8....56 B4
EXN EX4....15 F3
Bell St *BUD* EX9....53 G2
Belmont Rd *EX* EX1....3 F1
Belvedere Cl *TOP/EXT* EX3....35 H5
Belvedere Rd *EXM* EX8....56 B5
Belvidere Rd *EXN* EX4....15 F4
Bendarroch Rd *REXNE* EX5....21 E3
Bennett Cl *EXS* EX2....33 F3
Bennetts Hl *SID* EX10....38 B1
Bennett Sq *EXN* EX4....16 D5
Berkshire Dr *EXN* EX4....22 D4
Bernadette Cl *EXN* EX4....17 F5
Berrybrook Meadow
REXSW EX6....42 B3
Berry Cl *EXM* EX8....57 F4
Betjemen Dr *EXM* EX8....56 D1
Betony Ri *EXS* EX2....25 F5
Bettys Md *EXN* EX4....16 D5
Beverley Cl *EXS* EX2....25 E4
Bickleigh Cl *EXN* EX4....17 G3
Bickwell House La *SID* EX10....38 A3
Bickwell La *SID* EX10....38 B3
Bickwell Va *SID* EX10....38 B4
Bicton Pl *EX* EX1....3 J3
EXM EX8....62 B1
Bicton St *EXM* EX8....62 B1
Bicton Vls *EXM* EX8....62 C1
Biddington Wy *HON* EX14....4 C4
Bidmead Cl *EXM* EX8....57 F4
Bindon Rd *EXN* EX4....17 H3
Binford Cl *EX* EX1....25 E2
Birch Gv *OTT* EX11....21 F5
Birch Rd *EXM* EX8....50 C4
Birchwood Rd *EXM* EX8....57 E2
Birchy Barton Hl *EX* EX1....25 E2
Birdcage La *OTT* EX11....11 F4
Birkett Cl *EXS* EX2....25 F4
Bishops Cl *REXSW* EX6....55 E4
Bishops Court Gdns
REXNE EX5 *....26 D4
Bishop's Court La *REXNE* EX5....26 D5
Bishop Westall Rd *EXS* EX2....34 D1
Bittern Rd *EXS* EX2....25 H2
Blackall Rd *EXN* EX4....2 C1
Blackboy Rd *EXN* EX4....24 A1
Black Hat La *REXSW* EX6....22 A5
Blackhorse La *REXNE* EX5....18 C5
Blackmore Dr *SID* EX10....38 D4
Blackmore Rd *REXNE* EX5....37 G1
Blackthorn Cl *HON* EX14....5 E4
SID EX10....30 B5
Blackthorn Crs *EX* EX1....25 F2
Blenheim Rd *EXS* EX2....33 G1
Bluehayes La *REXNE* EX5....19 H2
Boarden Barn *EXM* EX8....62 C1
Bodley Cl *EX* EX1....25 E1
Bond's La *REXNE* EX5....45 F2
Bonfire La *REXNE* EX5....45 G3
Bonhay Cl *REXSW* EX6....55 E4
Bonhay Rd *EXN* EX4....23 F1
REXSW EX6....55 E4
Bonnington Gv *EX* EX1....3 J3
Bonville Cl *EX* EX1....25 E1
Booth Wy *EXM* EX8....56 C2
Border Rd *HON* EX14....4 B3
Boucher Rd *BUD* EX9....59 G3
Boucher Wy *BUD* EX9....59 G3
Boughmore La *SID* EX10....38 B5
Boughmore Rd *SID* EX10....38 B4
Bourn Ri *EXN* EX4....17 G3
Bovemoor's La *EXS* EX2....3 K5
Bowhay La *EXN* EX4....22 D4
Bowling Green Rd
TOP/EXT EX3....43 G2
Bowring Cl *EX* EX1....25 E1
Boyne Rd *BUD* EX9....59 F2
Bracken Cl *HON* EX14....4 B5
Brackendale *EXM* EX8....51 G5
Bracken Wy *DAW* EX7....60 D5
Brackenwood *EXM* EX8....56 D3
Bradfield Rd *EXN* EX4....17 G4
Bradford Cl *EXM* EX8....56 D1
Bradham Ct *EXM* EX8....57 E4
Bradham La *EXM* EX8....57 E4
Bradman Wy *EXS* EX2....33 G1
Bradninch Pl *EXN* EX4....2 B2
Bramble Cl *BUD* EX9....59 G3
SID EX10....30 D5
Bramble La *HON* EX14....4 D3
Bramley Av *EX* EX1....25 F2
Bramley Cl *REXSW* EX6....49 E5
Bramley Gdns *REXNE* EX5....10 A3
Brand Cl *HON* EX14....5 E4
Brand Rd *HON* EX14....5 E4
Branscombe Cl *EXN* EX4....22 D3
Brent Cl *REXNE* EX5....45 G3
Brenton Rd *REXSW* EX6....40 A4
Brentor Cl *EXN* EX4....15 E5
Breton Wy *EXM* EX8....57 F3
Bretteville Cl *REXNE* EX5....45 G3
Brewery La *SID* EX10....38 C3
Briar Cl *EXM* EX8....57 E4
HON EX14....5 E5
Briar Crs *EXS* EX2....34 C1
Brickyard La *REXSW* EX6....54 D4
Brickyard Rd *REXNE* EX5....20 C2
Bridespring Rd *EXN* EX4....16 C4
Bridford Rd *EXS* EX2....33 H1
Bridge Hl *TOP/EXT* EX3....43 F1
Bridgehill Garth
TOP/EXT EX3....43 F1

Bridge Rd *BUD* EX9....59 G2
 EXM EX8....56 B4
 REXSW EX6....34 C4
Bridge St *SID* EX10....31 F1
Brimpenny Rd *EXM* EX8....56 D3
Brittany Rd *EXM* EX8....56 D1
Britten Dr *EXS* EX2....25 E4
Brixington Dr *EXM* EX8....56 D3
Brixington La *EXM* EX8....56 D2
Brixington Parade Off
 Churchill Rd *EXM* EX8 *....57 E1
Broadfields Rd *EXS* EX2....25 F3
Broadgate *EX1*....2 B1
Broadleaf Cl *EX* EX1....17 H5
Broadmead *EXM* EX8....57 E2
 REXNE EX5....45 F3
Broadmeadow Av *EXN* EX4....23 E4
Broadoak Cl *OTT* EX11....21 F5
Broad Park Rd *EXM* EX8....56 D3
Broadparks Av *EXN* EX4....17 H3
Broadparks Cl *EXN* EX4....17 H3
Broad Vw *REXNE* EX5....9 F4
Broadway *EXS* EX2....23 E5
 REXNE EX5....45 G4
 SID EX10....38 B3
Broadway HI *EXS* EX2....22 D5
The Broadway *EXM* EX8....57 F4
Brodick Cl *EXN* EX4....16 A4
Brook Cl *EX* EX1....17 E5
 SID EX10....31 E4
Brookdale *OTT* EX11....13 E4
Brooke Av *EXS* EX2....24 C5
Brookfield Gdns *EXS* EX2....33 G3
Brookfield Rd *BUD* EX9....52 D4
Brook Green Ter *EXN* EX4 *....24 A1
Brookhayes Cl *EXM* EX8....56 C4
Brooklands Orch *OTT* EX11....13 E4
Brooklands Rd *EXM* EX8....57 E3
Brook La *SID* EX10....31 E4
Brookleigh Av *EX* EX1....25 E3
Brook Meadow *EXM* EX8....56 D3
 SID EX10....28 D5
Brook Rd *BUD* EX9....59 F4
Brookside *SID* EX10....38 C1
Brookside Crs *EXN* EX4....17 E4
Brook St *OTT* EX11....12 D5
Brookway *EX1*....24 D1
Broom Cl *EXS* EX2....24 D3
Browning Cl *EXS* EX2....24 D4
Brownlands Cl *SID* EX10....39 E3
Brownlands Rd *SID* EX10....39 E3
Brownlees *REXSW* EX6....42 A2
Brunel Cl *EXN* EX4....23 F1
Brunel Rd *REXSW* EX6....54 D1
Brunswick St *EXN* EX4....23 F3
Buchanan Cl *HON* EX14....4 C4
Buckerell Av *EXS* EX2....24 B5
Buckingham Cl *EXM* EX8....57 E5
Buckingham Rd *EXS* EX2....25 G5
Buckley Rd *SID* EX10....31 G3
Bucknill Cl *REXSW* EX6....42 A2
Buckton La *SID* EX10....31 H3
Buddle La *EXN* EX4....23 E3
Bude St *EXN* EX4....2 D2
Budlake Rd *EXS* EX2....33 H2
Budleigh HI *BUD* EX9....52 D4
Buller Rd *EXN* EX4....23 F3
Bull Meadow Rd *EXS* EX2....2 D5
Bulverton Pk *SID* EX10....38 B2
Bungalow La *EXS* EX2....2 E7
Bunn Rd *EXM* EX8....51 H5
The Buntings *REXSW* EX6....41 F2
Burch Cl *EXM* EX8....57 F2
Burgmanns HI *EXM* EX8....50 B4
The Burlands *HON* EX14....6 D2
Burnet Cl *EXS* EX2....25 F5
Burns Av *EXS* EX2....24 C5
Burnside *EXM* EX8....56 C3
Burnthouse La *EXS* EX2....24 C3
Burrator Dr *EXN* EX4....22 D1
Burrow Cl *SID* EX10....28 B5
Burrow La *SID* EX10....28 A5
Burrow Rd *REXNE* EX5....9 G3
Burscombe La *SID* EX10....30 C5
Buttery Cl *HON* EX14....5 E4
Buttery Rd *HON* EX14....5 E4
Butts Cl *HON* EX14....4 D4
Butt's HI *OTT* EX11....13 E4
Butts HI *REXSW* EX6....54 A1
Butts Rd *EXS* EX2....24 D3
 OTT EX11....13 E4
Byes Cl *SID* EX10....31 E5
Byeside Rd *SID* EX10....31 E5
Byes La *SID* EX10....31 F5
Byron Rd *EXS* EX2....25 F3
Byron Wy *EXM* EX8....56 D1
Bystock Cl *EXN* EX4....2 A1
Bystock Rd *EXM* EX8....51 H5
Bystock Ter *EXN* EX4....2 A1

C

Cadbury Gdns *BUD* EX9....52 D3
Cadhay La *OTT* EX11....12 B1
California Cl *EXN* EX4....16 A2
Calthorpe Rd *EXN* EX4....16 C5
Cambridge St *EXN* EX4....23 F3
Camelot Cl *EXN* EX4....16 D4
Camperdown Ter *EXM* EX8....61 H1
Campian Wy *HON* EX14....4 B5
Campion Gdns *EXS* EX2....25 E5
Canaan Cl *OTT* EX11....12 C3
Canal Banks *EXS* EX2....2 C7
Canberra Cl *EXN* EX4....16 B3
Canon Wy *EXS* EX2....33 G3
Canterbury Rd *EXN* EX4....22 D1
Capel La *EXM* EX8....57 G4
Capper Cl *SID* EX10....28 C5
Carberry Av *EXM* EX8....56 B3
Carlile Rd *EXS* EX2....24 D4
Carlton HI *EXM* EX8....62 B2
Carlton Rd *EXS* EX2....25 E4
Carlyon Cl *EX* EX1....24 D4
Carlyon Gdns *EX* EX1....24 D2
Caroline Cl *EX* EX1....57 E3
Carpenter Cl *EXN* EX4 *....2 A4
Carter Av *EXM* EX8....56 B4
Castle Farm *OTT* EX11....21 G4
Castle Ga *REXSW* EX6....54 B1
Castle Hill Vw *SID* EX10....31 F4
 REXNE EX5....45 G3
Castle La *EXN* EX4....57 H5
Castle Mt *EXN* EX4....23 G1
Castle St *EXN* EX4....2 C3
Cathedral Cl *EX* EX1....2 C3
Cathedral Yd *EXN* EX4....2 B3
Catherine St *EX* EX1....2 C3
Cauleston Cl *EXM* EX8....56 B2
Causey Gdns *EX* EX1....17 H4
Causey La *EX* EX1....18 A4
Cavendish Rd *EX* EX1....3 H2
Cecil Rd *EXS* EX2....23 H3
Cedar *DAW* EX7....60 D5
Cedar Cl *EXM* EX8....57 E1
 HON EX14....4 D3
Cedars Rd *EXS* EX2....2 D6
Celia Crs *EXN* EX4....16 D3
Cembra Cl *HON* EX14....5 F3
Central Av *EXN* EX4....17 E3
 EXS EX2....35 F4
Central Pl *HON* EX14....5 E2
Chamberlain Rd *EXS* EX2....2 B7
Chambers Cl *SID* EX10....30 C5
Chancel La *EXN* EX4....17 G4
Chancellor's Wy *EXN* EX4....16 D3
Chandlers' La *SID* EX10....38 D3
Chandlers Wk *EXS* EX2....2 C7
Chanter Ct *EXS* EX2 *....34 D1
Chantry Meadow *EXS* EX2....33 G3
Chapel HI *BUD* EX9....59 F3
 EXM EX8....62 B1
 TOP/EXT EX3....36 D5
Chapel La *OTT* EX11....13 E4
Chapel Pl *TOP/EXT* EX3 *....43 F2
Chapel Rd *EXM* EX8....50 B4
 EXS EX2....33 G2
 SID EX10....38 D5
Chapel St *BUD* EX9....59 F4
 EX EX1....2 C3
 EXM EX8....62 B1
 HON EX14....5 E2
 SID EX10....31 F2
 SID EX10....38 D5
Chapple Cl *REXSW* EX6....55 E4
Chard Rd *EX* EX1....24 D2
Chard Stock Cl *EX* EX1....25 G2
Charles Rd *HON* EX14....5 E2
Charles St *EXM* EX8....56 B5
Charlotte Ms *EXS* EX2 *....2 D4
Charnley Av *EXN* EX4....22 D3
The Chase *HON* EX14....5 F1
Chatham Cl *EXM* EX8....57 E4
Chaucer Av *EXS* EX2....24 C5
Chaucer Ri *EXM* EX8....56 D1
Cheeke St *EX* EX1....2 E2
Cheese La *SID* EX10....38 B4
Chelmsford Rd *EXN* EX4....22 D1
Cheltenham Cl *EXN* EX4....22 D1
Chepstow Cl *EXS* EX2....35 E3
Cheriswood Av *EXM* EX8....57 E3
Cherry Cl *EXM* EX8....56 D1
 HON EX14....4 B4
Cherry Gdns *EXS* EX2....24 D3
Cherry Tree Cl *EXM* EX8....15 F2
Cheshire Cl *EXM* EX8....57 F2
Chester Cl *EXN* EX4....22 D1
Chestnut Av *EXS* EX2....34 C1

Chestnut Cl *EXM* EX8....56 D1
Chestnut Cl *EXS* EX2....33 G3
Chestnut Wy *HON* EX14....4 C3
 SID EX10....28 D5
Cheynegate La *EXN* EX4....17 F3
Cheyne Ri *EXN* EX4....17 G3
Chichester Cl *EXM* EX8....56 D5
Chichester Ms *EX* EX1....2 D3
Chichester Wy *BUD* EX9....52 D3
Chineway Gdns *OTT* EX11....13 F5
Chineway Rd *OTT* EX11....13 G4
Chiverstone La *REXSW* EX6....48 C5
Chiverstone Rd *REXSW* EX6....48 C5
Christow Rd *EXS* EX2....33 G1
Chrystel Cl *SID* EX10....29 E1
Chudleigh Cl *EXS* EX2....33 G4
Chudley Cl *EXM* EX8....57 E4
Church Cl *REXNE* EX5....9 F3
Church HI *BUD* EX9....53 F2
 EXN EX4....17 G3
 HON EX14....5 F3
Churchill Cl *REXSW* EX6....54 B1
Churchill Rd *EXM* EX8....57 E2
 EXS EX2....23 E4
Church La *BUD* EX9....52 D3
 EXN EX4....17 G3
 EXS EX2....3 J5
 HON EX14....7 F2
 REXNE EX5....9 F3
 REXNE EX5....36 C2
Church Mews Off
 Little Bicton Pl *EXM* EX8 *....62 B1
Church Pth *TOP/EXT* EX3 *....43 F2
Church Path Rd *EXS* EX2....23 E5
Church Rd *EXM* EX8....50 C4
 EXS EX2....33 G1
 REXNE EX5....10 A3
 REXSW EX6....49 F4
 SID EX10....31 E4
Church Side *REXNE* EX5....27 E1
Church Stile *REXSW* EX6....42 B2
Church St *EXM* EX8....62 B1
 EXS EX2....3 K5
 REXSW EX6....54 A1
 SID EX10....31 E4
Church Ter *EXS* EX2....3 J4
Chute St *EX* EX1....3 F1
Clapperbrook La *EXS* EX2....33 G2
Clapper La *HON* EX14....5 E1
Clapps La *OTT* EX11....12 D5
Claredale Rd *EXM* EX8....62 C1
Claremont Gv *EXM* EX8....56 C5
 EXS EX2....2 E6
Claremont La *EXM* EX8....56 D5
Clarence Pl *EXN* EX4 *....24 A1
Clarence Rd *BUD* EX9....59 F3
 EXM EX8....56 B5
 EXS EX2....23 F3
Clarke Md *EXS* EX2....25 F4
Claylands Vw *HON* EX14....4 D4
Clay La *EXM* EX8....50 C5
Clayton Rd *EXS* EX2....23 F1
Clerk Cl *EXM* EX8....56 D2
Clevedon Cl *EXN* EX4....16 A4
Clevedon Pk *SID* EX10....39 E3
Cleveland Pl *EXM* EX8....62 A1
Cleveland St *EXN* EX4....23 F3
Cleve Rd *EXS* EX2....23 E2
Cliff Bastin Cl *EXS* EX2....25 F4
Clifford Cl *EX* EX1....25 E1
Clifford Rd *EXN* EX4....16 C5
Cliff Rd *SID* EX10....38 D5
Cliff Ter *BUD* EX9....59 F4
Clifton HI *EX* EX1....3 G1
Clifton Rd *EX* EX1....3 F2
Clifton St *EX* EX1....3 G2
Clinton Av *EXN* EX4....16 B5
Clinton Cl *BUD* EX9....59 E2
Clinton Sq *EXM* EX8....62 A1
Clinton St *EXN* EX4....23 F3
Clinton Ter *BUD* EX9....59 F2
Clipper Whf *EXM* EX8....61 H1
Cliston Av *EXN* EX4....57 E2
Cloister Garth *EX* EX1 *....2 C3
Cloister Rd *EXN* EX4....16 C5
The Cloisters *EX* EX1 *....2 C3
Clover Av *EXS* EX2....14 D5
Cludens Cl *EXS* EX2....33 G3
Clumpit La *REXSW* EX6....48 A5
Clydesdale Rd *EXN* EX4....16 A4
Clyst Av *REXNE* EX5....19 F3
Clyst Halt Av *EXS* EX2....25 H5
Clyst Heath *EXS* EX2....25 G4
Clyst Rd *TOP/EXT* EX3....36 C1
Clyst Valley Rd *REXNE* EX5....36 C2
Coastguard Rd *BUD* EX9....59 G3
Coastguard Rd *BUD* EX9....59 G4
Coates Rd *EXS* EX2....25 E3
Coburg Rd *SID* EX10....38 C5

Coburg Ter *SID* EX10....38 C5
Codrington St *EX* EX1....3 F2
Coffins La *REXSW* EX6....41 G2
Cofton HI *REXSW* EX6....60 D2
Cofton La *REXSW* EX6....60 C2
Cofton Rd *EXS* EX2....34 A3
Colands Ct *EXS* EX2....33 F3
Coleridge Cl *EXM* EX8....51 G5
Coleridge Rd *EXS* EX2....23 E4
 OTT EX11....13 F4
College Av *EXS* EX2....23 F4
College La *REXSW* EX6....32 A1
College Rd *EX* EX1....23 F4
The College *OTT* EX11....12 D4
Colleton Cl *EXS* EX2....56 D4
Colleton Crs *EXS* EX2....2 C5
Colleton Gv *EXS* EX2....2 D6
Colleton HI *EXS* EX2....2 C6
Colleton Ms *EXS* EX2....2 D6
Colleton Wy *EXS* EX2....56 D4
Collins Rd *EXN* EX4....16 A3
Colvin Cl *EXM* EX8....57 E5
Coly Rd *HON* EX14....5 E4
Combe Hayes *SID* EX10....30 D5
Comburg Cl *EXM* EX8....57 G1
Comilla Cl *EXM* EX8....56 D1
Commercial Rd *EXS* EX2....2 A5
Commin's Rd *EX* EX1....24 C1
Concorde Rd *EXM* EX8....57 F3
Conifer Ms *EXS* EX2 *....25 G5
Connaught Cl *SID* EX10....38 C4
Connaught Rd *SID* EX10....38 B4
Conrad Av *EXN* EX4....17 E5
Convent Flds *SID* EX10....38 B4
Convent Rd *SID* EX10....38 B4
Conybeare Cl *EXN* EX4....25 E1
Cookson's Rd *REXSW* EX6....54 D4
Coombe Cl *HON* EX14....5 E4
Coombe St *EX* EX1....2 C4
Copperfield Cl *EXM* EX8....57 F3
Copp Hill La *BUD* EX9....59 G3
Coppledown Gdns *BUD* EX9....59 E2
Coppledown Dr *EXN* EX4....15 F4
Copplestone Rd *BUD* EX9....59 F3
The Copse *EXM* EX8....57 F2
 EXS EX2....35 F4
 SID EX10....28 D5
Cordery Rd *EXS* EX2....23 E5
Core Flds *SID* EX10....30 D5
Core Hill Rd *SID* EX10....30 A2
Coreway *SID* EX10....30 D5
Coreway Cl *SID* EX10....30 C5
Coriolis Wy North *EX* EX1....25 G1
Cornflower HI *EXN* EX4....14 C5
Cornhill *OTT* EX11....13 E4
Corn Mill Crs *EXS* EX2....33 F2
Cornwall St *EXN* EX4....23 F3
Coronation Rd *EXS* EX2....24 D4
Coronet Cl *EXS* EX2....25 G5
Cotfield Cl *HON* EX14....5 E4
Cotfield St *EXS* EX2....23 H5
Cotford Rd *SID* EX10....31 G1
Cotlands *SID* EX10....38 B5
Cotmaton Rd *SID* EX10....38 B5
Cotterell Rd *REXNE* EX5....19 F3
Cottey Crs *EXN* EX4....16 D3
Cottington Md *SID* EX10....38 B4
Cottles La *REXNE* EX5....45 G2
Coulsdon Rd *SID* EX10....38 D2
Countess Wear Rd *EXS* EX2....34 C3
Counties Crs *REXSW* EX6....55 E4
Couper Mdw *EXS* EX2....25 C5
Courtenay *HON* EX14....4 C3
Courtenay Cl *REXSW* EX6....54 D4
Courtenay Gdns *EXS* EX2....33 F3
Courtenay Rd *EXS* EX2....23 G5
Courtenay Ter *REXSW* EX6....55 E4
Courtfield Ct *OTT* EX11....21 F5
Courtlands La *EXM* EX8....50 D5
Coventry Rd *EXN* EX4....23 E1
Coverdale Rd *EXS* EX2....23 C5
Cowick HI *EXS* EX2....23 E5
Cowick La *EXS* EX2....23 E5
Cowick Rd *EXS* EX2....23 F4
Cowick St *EXN* EX4....23 F4
Cowley Bridge Rd
 EXN EX4....15 E3
Cowley Vw *EXN* EX4 *....15 F4
Cowper Av *EXS* EX2....24 C5
Crabb La *EXS* EX2....33 E2
Cranbrook Rd *EXS* EX2....24 D3
Cranes La *BUD* EX9....52 D3
Cranford *SID* EX10....38 D3
Cranford Av *EXM* EX8....62 D1
Cranford Cl *EXM* EX8....62 D1
Cranford Vw *EXM* EX8....62 D1
Crawford Gdns *EXS* EX2 *....23 F5
Creely Cl *EXS* EX2....33 H3
The Crescent *EXM* EX8....57 F4

ricket Field La *BUD* EX9 ....59 F3
ricklepit Br *EXN* EX2 ....2 B5
richards *REXNE* EX5 ....45 G4
rockwells CI *REXSW* EX6 ....42 B3
rockwells Rd *REXSW* EX6 ....42 B3
roft Cha *EXN* EX4 ....22 D4
romwell Ter *EXS* EX2 ....25 G3
rosscut Wy *HON* EX14 ....5 E3
rossingfields Dr *EXM* EX8 ....56 B3
ross Vw *EXS* EX2 ....33 G2
rown Wy *EXS* EX2 ....25 G5
uckoo Down La *HON* EX14 ....5 G4
ulm CI *EXS* EX2 ....25 G4
ulm Gv *EXS* EX2 ....25 G4
ulverland CI *EXN* EX4 ....16 A5
ulverland Rd *EXN* EX4 ....16 A5
ulvery CI *REXNE* EX5 ....45 G3
umberland CI *EXM* EX8 ....57 E3
umberland Dr *EXS* EX2 ....25 G4
unningham Rd *EXM* EX8 ....57 E2
urie Ms *EXS* EX2 ....3 H7
urlew Wy *EXN* EX4 ....15 H3
utters Whf *EXM* EX8 * 61 H1
ypress CI *HON* EX14 ....4 B5
ypress Dr *EXS* EX2 ....23 E1
yprus Rd *EX8* 62 C1

D

Dagmar Rd *EXM* EX8 ....62 B1
Dairy CI *REXSW* EX6 ....42 B3
The Dairy Est *EXN* EX4 * 17 G4
Daisy Links *EXN* EX4 ....14 C5
Dalditch La *BUD* EX9 ....58 A1
Daleside Rd *EXN* EX4 ....16 A4
Danby La *EXM* EX8 ....56 B5
Danby Ter *EXM* EX8 ....56 B5
Dandy La *EXS* EX2 ....8 A5
Danes' Rd *EXN* EX4 ....23 C1
Danesway *EXN* EX2 ....17 H3
Dark La *BUD* EX9 ....59 E3
   SID EX10 ....38 B1
Darnell CI *SID* EX10 ....38 D2
Dawlish Rd *EXS* EX2 ....33 H4
Dawlish Warren Rd *DAW* EX7 ....61 E4
Dawn CI *EXN* EX4 ....24 D2
Days-Pottles La *EXS* EX2 ....41 E2
Deacon CI *EXS* EX2 ....33 G3
Deans Md *SID* EX10 ....38 C3
Dean St *EXS* EX2 ....2 D5
Deepdene Pk *EXS* EX2 ....3 G6
Deepway Gdns *REXSW* EX6 ....41 H2
Deepway La *EXS* EX2 ....41 F2
Deepway *BUD* EX9 ....58 D2
De La Rue Wy *EXN* EX4 ....17 G4
Delderfield Gdns *EXM* EX8 ....62 D1
Delius Crs *EXS* EX2 ....25 F3
Denbigh Ter *SID* EX10 ....38 D3
Denbury Ct *EXS* EX2 ....34 A3
Dene CI *EXM* EX8 ....57 E3
Dening Ct *EXM* EX8 ....56 C4
Denise CI *EXS* EX2 ....33 G3
Denmark Rd *EX* EX1 ....3 F1
   EXM EX8 ....57 E4
Dennedene CI *EXM* EX8 ....56 C1
Denver CI *TOP/EXT* EX3 ....36 A5
Denver Rd *TOP/EXT* EX3 ....35 H5
Devon Rd *EXN* EX4 ....16 C5
Devonshire Ct *HON* EX14 ....4 B4
Devon Shire PI *EXN* EX4 ....16 A5
Devonshire Rd *HON* EX14 ....4 A4
Diamond Rd *EXS* EX2 ....2 B6
Diane CI *EXM* EX8 ....51 H5
Dickens Dr *EXS* EX2 ....24 C5
Dick Pym CI *EXS* EX2 ....25 F4
Digby Dr *EXS* EX2 ....25 G5
Digby Rd *EXS* EX2 ....25 F5
Dinan Wy *EXM* EX8 ....51 G5
Dince Hill CI *REXNE* EX5 ....10 A2
Dinham CI *EX* EX1 ....23 F2
Dinham Ms *EXN* EX4 * 2 A3
Dinham Rd *EXN* EX4 ....2 A3
Dix's Fld *EX* EX1 ....2 D3
Dock Rd *EXM* EX8 ....62 A1
Dorchester Wy *EXM* EX8 ....51 H4
Doriam CI *EXS* EX2 ....15 H3
Dorset Av *EXN* EX4 ....22 D4
Dotton CI *EXS* EX2 ....25 G2
Douglas Av *EXM* EX8 ....62 C2
Dove CI *HON* EX14 ....4 D4
Dove La *SID* EX10 ....38 D5
Dove Wy *EXS* EX2 ....22 C5
Dowell St *HON* EX14 ....4 A4
Drake Av *EXS* EX2 * 25 G3
Drake's Av *EXM* EX8 ....57 E5
   SID EX10 ....31 E5
Drakes Farm *EXS* EX2 ....32 D1

Drakes Gdns *EXM* EX8 ....57 E4
Drakes Rd *EXN* EX4 ....23 F4
Draycott CI *EXS* EX2 ....24 D4
Drew's CI *REXSW* EX6 ....54 D4
Dreys Ct *EXS* EX2 ....3 H3
Dryden CI *EXM* EX8 ....56 D1
Dryden Rd *EXS* EX2 ....3 J7
Dryfield *REXSW* EX6 ....42 B2
Duchy Rd *HON* EX14 ....4 C4
Ducks Orch *REXSW* EX6 ....42 B3
Duckworth Rd *EXS* EX2 ....23 F5
Duke of Cornwall CI *EXM* EX8 ....57 F3
Dukes CI *BUD* EX9 ....53 C2
Dukes Crs *BUD* EX9 ....57 F3
Duke's Rd *BUD* EX9 ....59 E2
Dunning Ct *HON* EX14 ....4 D2
Dunrich CI *EXS* EX2 ....3 F4
Dunscombe La *SID* EX10 ....39 H2
Dunsford CI *EXM* EX8 ....63 E1
Dunsford Gdns *EXN* EX4 ....22 D5
Dunsford Rd *EXS* EX2 ....23 E5
Dunvegan CI *EXN* EX4 ....15 F5
Durbin CI *HON* EX14 ....5 F3
Durham CI *EX* EX1 ....25 F1
   EXM EX8 ....51 H5
Durham Wy *EXN* EX4 ....4 C4
Duryard Halls *EXN* EX4 * 15 F4

E

Eager Wy *REXSW* EX6 ....41 H1
Eagles Nest *EXS* EX2 ....22 C4
Eagle Wy *EXS* EX2 ....26 A3
Earl Richard's Rd North
   EXS EX2 ....24 B3
Earl Richard's Rd South
   EXS EX2 ....34 C1
East Av *EX* EX1 ....3 H1
East Budleigh Rd *BUD* EX9 ....59 G2
East Devon Wy *DAW* EX7 ....61 D5
   EXM EX8 ....60 D5
   SID EX10 ....29 H5
East Dr *EXM* EX8 ....56 B3
Eastern Av *EXS* EX2 ....35 F4
Eastfield *OTT* EX11 ....21 F4
Eastgate *EXN* EX4 ....2 C2
East Grove Rd *EXS* EX2 ....3 F5
East John Wk *EX* EX1 ....3 G2
East St *SID* EX10 ....38 D5
East Ter *BUD* EX9 ....59 G4
   EX EX1 * 24 D2
East Town La *REXSW* EX6 ....54 A1
East Wonford HI *EX* EX1 ....24 D3
Eaton Dr *EX* EX1 ....2 E2
Ebford La *TOP/EXT* EX3 ....44 A1
Ebrington Rd *EXS* EX2 ....23 C5
Edgbaston Md *EXS* EX2 ....25 F4
Edgerton Park Rd *EXN* EX4 ....15 H5
Edinburgh Crs *EXM* EX8 ....50 C3
Edinburgh Dr *EXN* EX4 ....22 D2
Edmonton CI *EXN* EX4 ....16 D5
Edmund St *EXS* EX2 ....2 A5
Edwards CI *EXS* EX2 ....25 G4
Egham Av *EXS* EX2 ....23 G5
Egremont Rd *EXM* EX8 ....56 B5
Elaine CI *EXS* EX2 ....16 D4
Eldertree Gdns *EXN* EX4 ....23 F1
Elgar CI *EXS* EX2 ....25 F3
Elim CI *SID* EX10 ....38 D3
Elizabeth Av *EXN* EX4 ....16 B5
Elizabeth CI *REXNE* EX5 ....10 A2
Elizabeth Rd *EXM* EX8 ....56 D2
Ellards CI *EXS* EX2 ....24 B5
Elliott CI *EXN* EX4 ....16 B3
Elliott Wy *EXS* EX2 ....25 C3
Ellwood Rd *EXM* EX8 ....57 E2
Elmbridge Gdns *EXN* EX4 ....15 F5
Elm CI *REXNE* EX5 ....9 F4
Elm Ct *REXSW* EX6 ....55 E4
Elmdon CI *EXN* EX4 ....16 A4
Elmfield Crs *EXM* EX8 ....56 B2
Elm Gv *EXM* EX8 ....62 A1
Elm Grove Av *TOP/EXT* EX3 ....43 F1
Elm Grove Gdns *TOP/EXT* EX3 ....43 F1
Elm Grove Rd *EXN* EX4 ....2 A1
   TOP/EXT EX3 ....43 F1
Elm La *EXM* EX8 ....57 C5
Elm Rd *EXM* EX8 ....56 C5
Elmside *BUD* EX9 ....59 F3
   EXN EX4 ....24 B1
Elmside CI *EXN* EX4 ....24 B1
Elm Wy *SID* EX10 ....30 D4
Elsdon La *OTT* EX11 ....21 G4
Elton Rd *EXN* EX4 ....16 B5
Elvis Rd *EXM* EX8 ....57 E5
Elwyn Rd *EXM* EX8 ....56 D5

Ely CI *EXN* EX4 ....22 C2
   HON EX14 ....6 D1
Elysian Flds *SID* EX10 ....38 C4
Emmanuel CI *EXN* EX4 ....23 F3
Emmanuel Rd *EXN* EX4 ....23 F3
Emmasfield *EXM* EX8 ....56 D5
Emperor Wy *EX* EX1 ....25 H2
Endfield CI *EX* EX1 ....25 E2
Endsleigh Crs *REXNE* EX5 ....26 C1
England's CI *SID* EX10 ....31 F4
Ennerdale Wy *EXN* EX4 ....23 E2
Ernsborough Gdns *HON* EX14 ....4 D3
Esplanade *EXM* EX8 ....62 A1
The Esplanade *SID* EX10 ....38 C5
Essex CI *EXN* EX4 ....22 D5
Essington CI *EXM* EX8 ....56 C1
Estuary Ct *EXM* EX8 ....61 H1
Estuary Vw *BUD* EX9 ....59 G3
Etonhurst CI *EXS* EX2 ....25 G5
Evergreen CI *EXM* EX8 ....57 E1
Evett CI *EXM* EX8 ....57 F4
Excalibur CI *EXN* EX4 ....16 D4
Exe St *EXN* EX4 ....2 A3
   TOP/EXT EX3 ....43 E1
Exeter CI *HON* EX14 ....6 D2
Exeter HI *REXSW* EX6 ....48 D5
Exeter Rd *DAW* EX7 ....60 B3
   EXM EX8 ....56 B5
   EXS EX2 ....35 G4
   HON EX14 ....4 B3
   OTT EX11 ....21 F1
   REXNE EX5 ....10 D5
   REXSW EX6 ....40 C4
   REXSW EX6 ....60 C2
   SID EX10 ....28 A5
Exe Vale Rd *EXS* EX2 ....34 D2
Exe Valley Wy *EXS* EX2 ....2 D1
Exe View Cots *EXN* EX4 * 15 E5
Exe View Rd *EXM* EX8 ....51 F3
Exhibition Wy *EXN* EX4 ....17 F4
Exminster HI *REXSW* EX6 ....42 B4
Exmouth Rd *BUD* EX9 ....58 D3
   EXM EX8 ....50 D3
   REXNE EX5 ....36 B1
   SID EX10 ....44 A3
Exton La *TOP/EXT* EX3 ....44 A4
Exton Rd *EXS* EX2 ....23 C5
Exwick Ct *EXN* EX4 ....15 E5
Exwick HI *EXN* EX4 ....22 D1
Exwick La *EXN* EX4 ....22 D1
Exwick Rd *EXN* EX4 ....23 E1
Eymore Dr *OTT* EX11 ....21 E4

F

Fairfax Gdns *EXS* EX2 ....33 G1
Fairfield Av *EXN* EX4 ....17 F5
Fairfield CI *EXM* EX8 ....62 C1
Fairfield Gdns *HON* EX14 ....4 D3
Fairfield Rd *EXM* EX8 ....62 C1
   EXS EX2 ....33 G3
Fairfield Ter *EXS* EX2 ....23 F4
Fairhazel Dr *EXN* EX4 ....23 E1
Fairlawn *SID* EX10 ....38 D3
Fairmead *SID* EX10 ....38 D3
Fairmead Ct *EX* EX1 * 17 H4
Fairpark CI *EXS* EX2 ....2 E5
Fairpark Rd *EXS* EX2 ....2 D5
Fairview Av *REXNE* EX5 ....37 E1
Fair View Rd *HON* EX14 ....5 E3
The Fairway *EXN* EX4 ....16 B4
Falcon Rd *EXS* EX2 ....25 H4
Falkland CI *EXN* EX4 ....16 A3
Farm CI *EXS* EX2 ....25 F4
Farm HI *EXN* EX4 ....14 C5
Farmhouse Av *EX* EX1 ....18 A5
Farm House Ri *REXSW* EX6 ....41 H2
Featherbed La *EXN* EX4 ....56 B2
Featherstone Rd *EXM* EX8 ....56 B2
Feltrim Av *EXS* EX2 ....24 A5
Fenny Br *HON* EX14 ....7 G3
Ferndale CI *HON* EX14 ....4 B4
Ferndale Rd *EXS* EX2 ....23 F4
Ferry Rd *TOP/EXT* EX3 ....43 F2
Filmer Wy *EXS* EX2 ....23 G5
Fingle CI *EXN* EX4 ....14 D5
Fir Tree CI *EXM* EX8 ....57 E5
Fire Beacon La *SID* EX10 ....29 H4
First Av *EX* EX1 ....3 J2
   EXS EX2 ....35 F4
The Firs *REXSW* EX6 ....46 C1
Fir Tree CI *EXM* EX8 ....57 G2
Fitzroy Rd *EX* EX1 ....25 H2
Fleming Av *SID* EX10 ....31 F5
Fleming Wy *EXS* EX2 ....3 H7
Florida Dr *EXN* EX4 ....16 A3

Flowerpot La *EXN* EX4 ....23 F3
Flower St *REXNE* EX5 ....45 G3
Follett Rd *TOP/EXT* EX3 ....43 E1
Ford Farm Ct *REXSW* EX6 * 54 A1
Ford La *OTT* EX11 ....21 F5
Fords Rd *EXS* EX2 ....2 B7
Fore St *BUD* EX9 ....53 E2
   BUD EX9 ....59 F4
   EX EX1 ....3 J4
   EXM EX8 ....62 B1
   EXN EX4 ....2 A2
   EXS EX2 ....32 D1
   REXSW EX6 ....54 A1
   SID EX10 ....31 F1
   SID EX10 ....38 D5
   TOP/EXT EX3 ....43 E1
Fore Street HI *BUD* EX9 ....59 G4
Forge CI *BUD* EX9 ....59 E2
Fortescue Rd *EXS* EX2 ....23 C5
   SID EX10 ....39 F1
Fortfield Ter *SID* EX10 ....38 C5
Forton Rd *EXM* EX8 ....56 D3
Fountain HI *BUD* EX9 ....59 E4
Fouracre CI *EXN* EX4 ....16 D4
Four Elms HI *SID* EX10 ....29 E5
Fowey CI *EX* EX1 * 24 C1
Fowler CI *REXSW* EX6 ....42 A2
Foxglove Ri *EXN* EX4 ....14 C5
Foxhayes Rd *EXN* EX4 ....23 C2
Foxholes HI *EXM* EX8 ....62 D3
Fox Rd *EXN* EX4 ....17 E3
Foxtor Rd *EXN* EX4 ....14 D5
Frances Gdns *EX* EX1 * 3 F2
Francis CI *EXN* EX4 ....23 F4
Franklea CI *OTT* EX11 ....12 D5
Franklin St *EXS* EX2 ....2 D5
Franklin CI *EXS* EX2 ....23 E5
Franklyn Dr *EXS* EX2 ....23 E5
Fraser Rd *EXM* EX8 ....57 E2
Freelands CI *EXM* EX8 ....57 E4
Frewins *BUD* EX9 ....59 E2
Friars' Ga *EXS* EX2 ....2 C5
Friars' Wk *EXS* EX2 ....2 C5
Friernhay St *EXN* EX4 ....2 A4
Frobisher Rd *EXM* EX8 ....56 D2
Frog La *REXNE* EX5 ....26 B5
Frogmore Rd *BUD* EX9 ....53 E3
Frog St *EXN* EX4 ....2 A5
Fry's La *SID* EX10 ....31 E4
Fulford Rd *EX* EX1 ....24 C1
Fulford Wy *REXSW* EX5 ....45 G4
Furzebrook *OTT* EX11 ....13 E4
Furze Rd *REXNE* EX5 ....45 F3

G

Galahad CI *EXN* EX4 ....16 D4
Gallery CI *HON* EX14 ....4 D2
Galmpton Ri *EXN* EX4 ....16 B3
Galsworthy Sq *EXN* EX4 ....17 E5
Gandy St *EXN* EX4 ....2 B2
Garden CI *EXS* EX2 ....25 F4
Gareth Crs *EXN* EX4 ....16 C3
Garland CI *EXN* EX4 ....14 C5
Garratt CI *EXM* EX8 ....56 D1
Gater La *EX* EX1 ....2 C4
Generals CI *REXSW* EX6 ....54 D5
Generals La *REXSW* EX6 ....55 E5
Geneva CI *EXN* EX4 ....3 H6
Georges CI *EX* EX1 ....25 E2
George St *EX* EX1 ....2 B4
   EXM EX8 ....56 B5
   HON EX14 ....5 E2
Gervase Av *EXS* EX2 ....2 A6
Gibraltar Rd *EXM* EX8 ....50 C3
Gibson CI *EXM* EX8 ....57 F3
Gilbert Av *EXS* EX2 ....25 F4
Gilchrist Wy *SID* EX10 ....39 E3
Gipsy Hill La *EX* EX1 ....18 A5
Gipsy La *EXM* EX8 ....56 B5
Gissage Vw *HON* EX14 ....4 D2
Gissons Rd *EXS* EX2 ....42 B2
Gissons La *REXSW* EX6 ....46 C1
Gittisham CI *EXS* EX2 ....25 G2
Gladstone Rd *EX* EX1 ....3 G3
Glanvill Wy *HON* EX14 ....4 D4
Glasshouse La *EXS* EX2 ....34 D3
Glastonbury CI *EXN* EX4 ....16 D3
Glave Saunders Av *EXS* EX2 ....25 F4
Glebe CI *BUD* EX9 ....53 G2
   SID EX10 ....50 C3
Glebelands *EXM* EX8 ....50 C3
   REXSW EX6 ....42 A2
   SID EX10 ....28 D5
   SID EX10 ....38 C4
Glen CI *REXNE* EX5 ....37 F1
   SID EX10 ....38 C5

Glen Farm Crs HON EX14 .....5 F3
Glenisla Ter SID EX10 .....38 D5
Glenmore Rd EX EX1 .....24 D3
Glen Rd SID EX10 .....38 C5
Glenthorne Rd EXN EX4 .....15 H4
Glenview HON EX14 .....5 F3
Glenwood Ri EXS EX2 .....2 E7
Globefield TOP/EXT EX3 .....43 F1
Globe Hl REXNE 45 F3
Globe La TOP/EXT EX3 .....43 F2
Gloucester Cl HON EX14 .....4 C3
Gloucester Crs HON EX14 .....4 C3
Gloucester Rd EXM EX8 .....57 E1
   EXN EX4 .....22 D2
Goldsmith St EX EX1 .....3 J2
Gold St OTT EX11 .....12 D5
Good Shepherd Dr EXS EX2 .....2 C5
Gordon Rd EX EX1 .....3 G1
   TOP/EXT EX3 .....35 H5
Gordon's Pl EXS EX2 .....3 K4
Gore La EXM EX8 .....63 F3
Gorfin Cl EXM EX4 .....57 F4
Gorse La EX EX1 .....51 H5
Gorse Wy SID EX10 .....38 B4
Gosceline Wk HON EX14 .....5 E4
Gosford Av OTT EX11 .....12 C1
Gosford Rd OTT EX11 .....12 D1
Govetts REXNE 45 G3
Grace Road Central EXS EX2 .....33 H1
Grace Rd South EXS EX2 .....34 A2
Grace Rd West EXS EX2 .....33 G1
Grafton Rd EX EX4 .....15 F4
Grainger Cl EXS EX2 .....25 F3
Granary La BUD EX9 .....59 H2
Grandisson Dr OTT EX11 .....13 E5
Grange Av EXM EX8 .....56 C3
Grange Cl EXM EX8 .....50 D4
   EXM EX8 .....56 C3
Gras Lawn EXS EX2 .....24 B5
Grasslands Dr EX EX1 .....17 H5
Great Hill Vw EXN EX4 .....16 B2
Greatwood Ter TOP/EXT EX3 .....43 F1
Grecian Wy EXS EX2 .....25 F4
Green Cl EXM EX4 .....56 D4
Greendale La REXNE EX5 .....37 H3
Greenford Vls EXS EX2 .....2 B6
Greenhead SID EX10 .....30 D1
Greenhill Av EXM EX8 .....50 C4
   EXM EX8 .....56 D5
Green La EXN EX4 .....22 D3
   TOP/EXT EX3 .....43 H4
Green Mt SID EX10 .....39 E3
Greenpark Av EX EX1 .....25 G1
Greenpark Rd EXM EX8 .....57 E2
The Green EXM EX8 .....56 D5
   EXS EX2 .....32 C2
   REXNE EX5 .....10 A2
Green Tree La REXNE EX5 .....9 G4
Greenway EXS EX2 .....25 F4
   REXNE EX5 .....45 G3
Greenway La BUD EX9 .....59 E2
   SID EX10 .....29 G5
Grenadier Rd EX EX1 .....25 H1
Grendon Blds EX EX1 * 2 B4
Grendon Rd EX EX1 .....3 H3
Grenville Av EXM EX8 .....17 F5
Grenville Rd EXM EX8 .....56 D2
Greyfriars Rd EXM EX4 .....16 C5
Grigg's La EXM EX8 .....39 F1
Grindle Wy REXNE EX5 .....36 C1
Gronau Cl HON EX14 .....5 E4
Grosvenor Pl EX EX1 .....3 H2
Grove Hl TOP/EXT EX3 .....43 F1
Grove Rd REXNE EX5 .....10 B2
The Grove SID EX10 .....38 D4
Guildford Cl EXM EX4 .....22 D2
Guinea St EX EX1 .....2 B4
Guinevere Wy EXM EX4 .....16 D4
Guinness La EXN EX4 .....14 D5
Gussiford La EXM EX8 .....62 B1
Guys Rd EXN EX4 .....23 E2

H

Haccombe Cl EXN EX4 .....22 D3
Haddeo Dr EXS EX2 .....25 G4
Hadrian Dr EX EX1 .....25 H1
Hadrians Wy EXM EX8 .....57 E3
Haldon Cl TOP/EXT EX3 .....35 H5
Haldon Rd EXN EX4 .....23 F2
Haldon View Ter EXS EX2 .....3 H5
Hale La HON EX14 .....5 F2
Halscombe La EXS EX2 .....32 B2
Halsdon Av EXM EX8 .....56 B4
Halsdon Cl EXM EX8 .....56 B4
Halsdon Rd EXM EX8 .....56 B5

Halse Hl BUD EX9 .....59 E3
Halses Cl EXN EX4 .....14 C5
The Halt EXS EX2 .....33 G2
Halyards EX EX1 * 61 H1
Hambeer La EXS EX2 .....22 D5
Hamilton Av EXS EX2 .....34 C1
Hamilton Dr EXS EX2 .....25 C3
Hamilton Gv REXSW EX6 .....55 E5
Hamilton Rd EXM EX8 .....56 D5
   EXS EX2 .....57 E5
   TOP/EXT EX3 .....35 H5
Ham La SID EX10 .....38 D5
Hamlin Gdns EX EX1 .....24 D1
Hamlin La EX EX1 .....24 D2
Hammond Croft Wy EXS EX2 .....33 G3
Hampden Pl EXS EX2 * 2 A6
Hampshire Cl EXN EX4 .....22 D4
The Hams EXS EX2 .....32 C2
Hanover Cl EX EX1 .....3 J1
Hanover Rd EX EX1 .....3 J2
Hansford Wy OTT EX11 .....12 C5
Harbour Ct EXM EX8 .....62 A1
Harcombe Flds SID EX10 .....31 F5
Harcombe La SID EX10 .....31 F5
Harcombe La East SID EX10 .....31 G5
Hardy Rd EXS EX2 .....25 G3
Harebell Copse EXN EX4 .....14 C5
Harefield Cl EXN EX4 .....15 F5
Harefield Dr EXM EX8 .....50 D4
Harefield Rd EXM EX8 .....51 E3
Harpford Br SID EX10 .....28 D4
Harrier Wy EXS EX2 .....25 H4
Harringcourt Rd EXN EX4 .....17 H3
Harrington Dr EXN EX4 .....17 H3
Harrington Gdns EXN EX4 .....17 H4
Harrington La EXN EX4 .....17 G3
Hartley Rd EXM EX8 .....62 B1
Hartopp Rd EXM EX8 .....56 B5
Harts Cl EX EX1 .....17 H5
Hart's La EX EX1 .....17 C5
Harwood Cl EXM EX8 .....57 E3
Hatcher Cl HON EX14 .....5 C5
Hatchland Rd EXN EX4 .....8 C4
Hatherleigh Rd EXS EX2 .....33 F1
Hatway Hl SID EX10 .....31 G1
Haven Banks EXS EX2 .....2 C6
Haven Cl EXS EX2 .....2 B7
Haven Rd EXS EX2 .....2 A6
Hawkins La OTT EX11 .....21 F5
Hawthorn Cl HON EX14 .....4 D3
Hawthorn Dr SID EX10 .....30 B5
Hawthorn Gv EXM EX8 .....57 F2
Hawthorn Rd EXS EX2 .....24 C5
Hawthorn Wy EXS EX2 .....33 F3
Haydons Pk HON EX14 .....5 E3
Hayes Barton Ct EXN EX4 .....23 F3
Hayes Cl BUD EX9 .....59 F2
Hayes La BUD EX9 .....52 B2
Hayeswood La BUD EX9 .....52 C3
Hayne Cl EXN EX4 .....24 D1
   SID EX10 .....29 E1
Hayne Hl SID EX10 .....29 E3
Hayne La HON EX14 .....4 B5
Hayne Pk SID EX10 .....29 E1
Haytor Dr EXN EX4 .....22 D1
Hazel Cl SID EX10 .....28 D5
Hazeldene Gdns EXM EX8 .....56 B3
Hazelmead Rd REXNE EX5 .....37 E1
Hazel Rd EXS EX2 .....34 C1
Hazelwood Cl HON EX14 .....5 E4
Hazelwood Dr DAW EX7 .....60 D5
Headland Cl EX EX1 .....25 F1
Headland Crs EX EX1 .....25 F1
Headon Gdns EXS EX2 .....34 D2
Heard Av EXM EX8 .....57 F4
Heath Cl HON EX14 .....4 B4
Heather Cl EXS EX2 .....25 E2
   HON EX14 .....4 B5
Heatherdale EXM EX8 .....62 D1
Heather Gra OTT EX11 .....21 F5
Heathpark Wy HON EX14 .....4 B3
Heath Rd EXS EX2 .....25 E4
Heavitree Pk EXS EX2 .....24 D3
Heavitree Rd EX EX1 .....3 F3
Hele Rd EXN EX4 .....23 F1
Hellier Cl EXN EX4 .....4 C4
Hellings Gdns REXNE EX5 .....9 F3
Heneaton Sq EXS EX2 .....35 E3
Henley Rd EXM EX8 .....56 D5
Hennock Road Central EXS EX2 .....33 H2
Hennock Rd East EXS EX2 .....33 H2
Hennock Rd North EXS EX2 .....33 H1
Hensleigh Dr EXS EX2 .....3 G4
Heraldry Wy EXN EX4 .....25 G4
Herbert Rd EX EX1 .....24 C1
Hereford Cl EXM EX8 .....51 H5
Heritage Wy SID EX10 .....30 D5
Heron Rd EXS EX2 .....22 C5

   EXS EX2 .....25 H3
   HON EX14 .....4 D4
Herschell Rd EXN EX4 .....16 B5
Hexworthy Av EXN EX4 .....14 D5
Heywood Dr REXSW EX6 .....54 D4
Hickory Cl EXN EX4 .....5 G3
Hides Rd SID EX10 .....31 E5
Highbury Pk EXM EX8 .....56 B3
Highcliffe Cl EXM EX8 .....50 B5
Highcroft EXN EX4 .....15 F4
Highcross Rd EXN EX4 .....23 H1
Higher Aboveway REXSW EX6 .....42 B3
Higher Barley Mt EXN EX4 .....22 D3
Higher Bedlands BUD EX9 .....59 E2
Higher Brand La EXS EX2 .....5 E5
Higher Brook Meadow SID EX10 .....31 E4
Higher Down REXSW EX6 .....54 A1
Higher Duryard EXN EX4 * 15 H3
Higher Exwick Hl EXN EX4 .....22 D1
Higher Fortescue OTT EX11 .....39 F2
Higher Greenway La SID EX10 .....38 C3
Higher Hill Vw SID EX10 .....38 C3
Higher Hoopern La EXN EX4 .....15 H4
Higher King's Av EXN EX4 .....16 A4
Higher Ridgeway OTT EX11 .....13 E4
Higher Shapter St TOP/EXT EX3 .....43 F2
Higher Spring Gdns OTT EX11 .....13 E5
Higher Summerlands EX EX1 * 3 G2
Higher Wy EXS EX2 .....29 E4
Higher Wear Rd EXS EX2 .....35 F4
Higher Woolbrook Pk SID EX10 .....38 B1
Highfield HON EX14 .....4 D3
   TOP/EXT EX3 .....36 A4
Highfield La EXM EX8 .....62 C1
High Meadow SID EX10 .....38 C1
High Mdw EXN EX4 .....22 D3
High St BUD EX9 .....59 F4
   EXM EX8 .....2 B3
   EXN EX4 .....32 C2
   HON EX14 .....4 D3
   REXSW EX6 .....54 A1
   SID EX10 .....28 C5
   SID EX10 .....38 D4
   TOP/EXT EX3 .....35 H5
High Vw HON EX14 .....6 D2
Hill Barton Cl EX EX1 .....25 F1
Hill Barton La EX EX1 .....25 F1
Hill Barton Rd EX EX1 .....25 F1
Hill Cl EXN EX4 .....16 A4
Hill Crs HON EX14 .....5 F2
Hill Crest REXSW EX6 .....42 A4
Hillcrest Pk EXN EX4 .....15 H3
Hill Dr EXM EX8 .....56 C1
Hill La EX EX1 .....25 E1
Hill Ri EX EX1 .....25 F1
Hillsborough Av EXN EX4 .....23 H1
Hillside SID EX10 .....28 B5
Hillside Av EXN EX4 .....23 H1
Hillside Rd SID EX10 .....38 D4
Hill Vw SID EX10 .....38 D3
Hillyfield Rd EX EX1 .....25 F1
Hind St OTT EX11 .....12 D5
Hoker Rd EXS EX2 .....24 D4
Holcombe La OTT EX11 .....13 F2
Holland Rd EXM EX8 .....57 E3
   EXS EX2 .....23 E4
Holley Cl REXSW EX6 .....42 A4
Hollis Cl OTT EX11 .....13 E4
Holloway St EXS EX2 .....2 C5
Hollow La EX EX1 .....25 G1
Hollow Pits Ct EXS EX2 .....33 G3
The Hollows EXM EX8 .....56 C5
Holly Cl HON EX14 .....5 G2
   REXNE EX5 .....9 F3
Hollymount Cl EXM EX8 .....56 D1
Holly Rd EXS EX2 .....24 C5
Holly Wk EXM EX8 .....57 E1
Holman Wy TOP/EXT EX3 .....43 F2
Holmdale SID EX10 .....38 D4
Holne Ct EXS EX2 .....14 D5
Holne Ri EXS EX2 .....25 E4
The Holt HON EX14 .....5 G2
Homefield Cl OTT EX11 .....13 E5
Homefield Rd EX EX1 .....3 J3
Honeylands Dr EXN EX4 .....24 D1
Honey La EX EX1 .....18 A3
Honey Park Rd BUD EX9 .....59 G2
Honeysuckle Ct EXS EX2 .....14 C5
Honeysuckle Dr HON EX14 .....4 B5
Honiton Rd EXS EX2 .....25 F3
Hooker Cl BUD EX9 .....53 G2
Hoopern Av EXN EX4 .....15 H4
Hoopern La EXN EX4 .....15 H5
Hoopern St EXN EX4 .....23 G1

Hope Pl EXS EX2 * 24 D3
Hope Rd EXS EX2 .....24 D3
Hornbeam Cl HON EX14 .....4 D4
Horseguards EX EX1 .....23 H1
Hospital La EX EX1 .....17 F5
Houndbeare La REXNE EX5 .....20 B5
Howard Cl EX EX1 .....15 G5
Howarth Cl SID EX10 .....30 C5
Howell Rd EXN EX4 .....23 G1
Hulham Rd EXM EX8 .....56 C1
Hulham V EXM EX8 .....56 D2
Hummingbird Cl EXN EX4 .....17 H4
Hungry Fox Est REXNE EX5 .....19 F2
Hunton Cl EXM EX8 .....50 C4
Hurst Av EXS EX2 .....25 H1
Hutchings Md EX EX1 .....18 A4
Hylands Cl OTT EX11 .....21 F5
Hylton Gdns EXN EX4 .....23 E2

I

Ice House La SID EX10 .....38 D1
Iddesleigh Rd EXN EX4 .....16 B5
Ide La EXS EX2 .....33 G3
Ilex Cl EXN EX4 .....17 E3
   EXS EX2 .....40 A2
Imperial Rd EXM EX8 .....62 A1
Imperial St EXN EX4 .....23 H1
Inner Ting Tong BUD EX9 .....58 B1
Iolanthe Dr EXN EX4 .....5 G3
Iona Av EXM EX8 .....56 B2
Iris Av EXS EX2 .....2 A6
Isaac Cl BUD EX9 .....53 G2
Isambard Pde EXN EX4 .....23 F1
Isca Rd EXM EX8 .....62 D1
   EXS EX2 .....2 B7
Isleworth Rd EXN EX4 .....22 D3
Ivy Cl EXS EX2 .....24 D4
   SID EX10 .....38 D1
Ivydale EXM EX8 .....57 E1

J

Jacketts BUD EX9 .....53 G2
James Owen Ct EXN EX4 .....24 A1
Jarvis Cl EXM EX8 .....57 E3
Jennifer Cl EXS EX2 .....5 E3
Jerrard Cl HON EX14 .....5 E3
Jerrard Rd EXS EX2 .....23 C5
Jesmond Rd EXN EX4 .....24 B1
Jesu St OTT EX11 .....12 D5
Jocelyn Rd BUD EX9 .....59 F2
John Levers Wy EXN EX4 .....23 E2
John St EXN EX4 .....2 B4
Joslin Rd EXN EX4 .....4 C4
Jubilee Cl REXSW EX6 .....42 B3
Jubilee Dr EXN EX4 .....56 D1
Jubilee Gdns SID EX10 .....31 E5
Jubilee Rd EXN EX4 .....24 B1
Juniper Cl EXN EX4 .....17 E3
   HON EX14 .....4 C4
Jupes Cl REXSW EX6 .....42 B3

K

Katherines La OTT EX11 .....13 E4
Kay Cl EXM EX8 .....56 D4
Keats Cl EXM EX8 .....51 C5
Kenbury Crs REXSW EX6 .....61 E2
Kenbury Dr EXS EX2 .....33 H3
Kendall Cl EXN EX4 * 24 A1
Kennaway Rd OTT EX11 .....13 E4
Kennerley Av EXN EX4 .....17 E5
Kennford Rd EXS EX2 .....23 C5
Kenn La REXSW EX6 .....41 H5
Kent Cl EXS EX2 .....24 D4
Kenton Hl REXSW EX6 .....54 A1
Kenton Ms REXSW EX6 .....54 A1
Kersbrook La BUD EX9 .....59 F1
Kerslake's Ct HON EX14 .....5 E2
Kerswill Rd EXN EX4 .....23 E4
Kestell Rd SID EX10 .....39 E4
Kestor Dr EXN EX4 .....14 D5
Kestrel Wy EXS EX2 .....25 H3
Keverel Rd EXM EX8 .....56 B3
Kilbarran Ri EXN EX4 .....15 F5
Kimberley Rd EXS EX2 .....2 D5
King Alfred Wy SID EX10 .....28 C5
King Arthur's Rd EXN EX4 .....16 C3
King Charles Wy SID EX10 .....30 D5
Kingdom Ms EXN EX4 .....23 F1
King Edward St EXN EX4 .....15 H4

Kingfisher Dr *EXN* EX4 ....16 A3
Kingfisher La *EXS* EX2 ....22 C5
King Henry's Rd *EXS* EX2 ....34 B1
Kings Av *OTT* EX11 ....13 F4
Kings Ct *HON* EX14 ....5 E2
Kings Dwellings *EX1* * 2 B4
Kingsgate *EXN* EX4 * 16 A5
Kingslake Rise Off Mudbank La
    EXM * 56 B4
Kings La *SID* EX10 ....38 D5
Kingsley Av *EXN* EX4 ....17 G5
King's Rd *EXN* EX4 ....16 B5
    HON EX14 ....5 F2
Kingstephen Cl *EXN* EX4 ....23 H1
Kingston Rd *EXM* EX8 ....56 D5
Kingsway *EXS* EX2 ....3 K5
Kingswood Cl *EXN* EX4 ....14 D5
King William St *EX1* 2 D1
Kinnerton Wy *EXN* EX4 ....14 C5
Kipling Dr *EXS* EX2 ....3 K7
Knapp Hl *SID* EX10 ....38 C3
Knapp's La *SID* EX10 ....29 E3
Knightley Rd *EXS* EX2 ....24 B5
Knights Crs *EXS* EX2 ....25 C5
Knightstone La *OTT* EX11 ....13 F5
Knowle Cl *HON* EX14 ....5 E2
Knowle Dr *EXN* EX4 ....23 E1
    SID EX10 ....38 B4
Knowle Gdns *SID* EX10 ....38 B4
Knowle Hl *BUD* EX9 ....58 C3
Knowle Rd *BUD* EX9 ....58 D2

L

Laburnum Cl *EXM* EX8 ....57 E1
    HON EX14 ....4 B4
Laburnum Rd *EXS* EX2 ....24 C5
Lackaborough Ct *EXS* EX2 ....33 F3
Ladmead *SID* EX10 ....30 B5
Ladysmith Rd *EX1* 3 J1
Lake Cl *HON* EX14 ....5 F3
Lakelands Dr *EXN* EX4 ....23 E2
Lakeside *DAW* EX7 ....60 D5
Lakeside Av *EXS* EX2 ....35 E3
Lamacraft Dr *EXN* EX4 ....24 D1
Lamplough Rd *EXM* EX8 ....56 B1
Lancaster Cl *EXS* EX2 ....25 E3
Lancelot Rd *EXN* EX4 ....16 D3
Landhayes Rd *EXN* EX4 ....23 E3
Landscore Rd *EXN* EX4 ....23 E3
Lands Rd *EXN* EX4 ....17 G4
Langaton Gdns *EX1* 18 A4
Langaton La *EX1* 18 A4
Langerwehe Wy *EXM* EX8 ....62 A1
Langford Av *HON* EX14 ....5 F2
Langford Rd *HON* EX14 ....5 F1
Langland La *OTT* EX11 ....12 E3
Langstone Dr *EXM* EX8 ....56 D2
Lansdowne *EXS* EX2 * 25 E4
Lansdowne Rd *BUD* EX9 ....58 C3
Lansdowne Ter *EXS* EX2 ....2 B5
Larch Cl *EXM* EX8 ....56 D1
Larch Rd *EXS* EX2 ....23 E5
Larkbeare Av *REXNE* EX5 ....11 G2
Larkbeare Rd *EXS* EX2 ....2 D6
Lark Cl *EXN* EX4 ....16 A4
Lark Ri *SID* EX10 ....28 C5
Laskeys La *SID* EX10 ....39 E4
Latimer Rd *EXN* EX4 ....16 D5
Laurel Ri *EXM* EX8 ....57 E4
Laurel Rd *EXS* EX2 ....24 C5
    HON EX14 ....4 B4
Lavender Rd *EXN* EX4 ....14 D5
Lawn Rd *EXM* EX8 ....56 B5
The Lawn *BUD* EX9 ....59 F4
Lawn Vis *SID* EX10 ....38 D3
Lawrence Av *EXN* EX4 ....23 F3
Laxton Av *EX1* 25 F5
Lea Rd *BUD* EX9 ....53 C2
Leas Rd *BUD* EX9 ....59 F5
Lebanon Cl *EXN* EX4 ....16 B4
Lee Cl *HON* EX14 ....4 D2
Legion Wy *EXS* EX2 ....33 G2
Leicester Md *EXS* EX2 ....22 D1
Leighdene Cl *EXS* EX2 ....3 G6
Leighton Ter *EX1* 2 D1
Le Locle Cl *SID* EX10 ....30 B5
Lennox Av *SID* EX10 ....30 D4
Leslie Rd *EXM* EX8 ....56 B4
Lestock Cl *EXM* EX8 ....57 F5
Lethbridge Rd *EXS* EX2 ....25 E3
Lewis Crs *EXS* EX2 ....25 C5
Leypark Cl *EX1* 25 F1

Leypark Crs *EX1* 25 F2
Leypark Rd *EX1* 25 F1
Lichfield Rd *EXN* EX4 ....22 C2
Lichgate Rd *EXS* EX2 ....33 G3
Liffey Ri *EXN* EX4 ....14 D5
Lilac Rd *EXS* EX2 ....24 C5
Lilley Wk *HON* EX14 ....5 F3
Lily Mt *EX1* 14 C5
Lime Cl *REXNE* EX5 ....9 F4
Lime Gv *EXM* EX8 ....56 D1
    REXSW EX6 ....42 A1
Limegrove Rd *EXN* EX4 ....23 E3
Lime Kiln La *EXS* EX2 ....34 D2
Lime Tree Cl *EXS* EX2 ....25 F5
Lincoln Cl *EXM* EX8 ....51 H5
    HON EX14 ....6 D1
Lincoln Rd *EXN* EX4 ....22 D2
Linda Cl *EX1* 25 F3
Linden Cl *EXM* EX8 ....56 D2
Linden V *EXN* EX4 * 23 G1
Linfield Gdns *EXN* EX4 ....23 E4
Linhay Cl *HON* EX14 ....4 D5
Links Rd *BUD* EX9 ....58 D4
Linnet Cl *EXN* EX4 ....16 A3
Lisa Cl *EXS* EX2 ....24 D4
Lister Cl *EXS* EX2 ....3 H7
Little Bicton Pl *EXM* EX8 ....62 B1
Littledown La *EXM* EX8 ....57 G5
Littleham Rd *EXM* EX8 ....57 F5
Little John's Cross Hl *EXS* EX2 ...22 D5
Little Knowle *BUD* EX9 ....59 E3
Littlemead La *EXM* EX8 ....56 B1
Little Meadow *EXM* EX8 ....57 E1
Little Queen St *EX1* 2 C2
Little Rack St *EX1* 2 B4
Little Silver *EX1* 2 A2
Little Silver La *EXS* EX2 ....41 F1
Littletown Rd *HON* EX14 ....4 D4
Littleway *EXS* EX2 ....23 E5
Livermore Rd *EXM* EX8 ....5 E3
Liverpool Hl *EXN* EX4 ....22 D1
Liverton Cl *EXM* EX8 ....57 F4
Livonia Rd *SID* EX10 ....39 E2
Lloyds Ct *EX1* 17 F5
Lloyds Crs *EX1* 25 F1
Locarno Rd *EXN* EX4 ....22 D4
Lock Cl *SID* EX10 ....30 C5
Locksley Cl *EXN* EX4 ....34 D3
Lockyer Av *SID* EX10 ....31 E5
Lodge Hl *EX1* 15 F5
Longbrook La *EXM* EX8 ....50 D5
Longbrook St *EXN* EX4 ....2 D1
Longbrook Ter *EX1* 2 D1
Long Cswy *EXM* EX8 ....62 C1
Long Copp *BUD* EX9 ....59 F2
Longdogs La *OTT* EX11 ....13 E5
Longdown Rd *EXS* EX2 ....22 A5
Longfield Est *REXSW* EX6 ....54 D4
Long La *EXM* EX8 ....62 D1
Longfield Est ...
Longmeadow Rd *EXM* EX8 ....50 D4
Long Pk *REXNE* EX5 ....45 G3
Lonsdale Rd *EX1* 24 D3
Looe Rd *EXN* EX4 ....23 F1
Loram Wy *EXS* EX2 ....33 H3
Lords Wy *EXS* EX2 ....25 F4
Louisa Pl *EXM* EX8 ....62 B1
Louisa Ter *EXM* EX8 ....62 B2
Louvigny Cl *HON* EX14 ....6 D2
Lovelace Crs *EXM* EX8 ....57 E4
Lovelace Gdns *EXS* EX2 ....33 G3
Lovell Cl *EXM* EX8 ....56 D1
Lovering Cl *EXM* EX8 ....56 D1
Lower Albert St *EX1* 3 F2
Lower Argyll Rd *EXN* EX4 ....15 F4
Lower Av *EX1* 3 J2
Lower Brand La *HON* EX14 ....5 E4
Lower Broad Oak Rd *OTT* EX11 ...21 G4
Lower Brook Meadow
    SID 31 E4
Lower Budleigh *BUD* EX9 ....52 D4
Lower Coombe St *EX1* 2 B5
Lower Duck St *REXSW* EX6 ....42 B3
Lower Fore St *EXM* EX8 ....62 B1
Lower Griggs *SID* EX10 ....39 F1
Lower Harrington La *EXN* EX4 .....17 H4
Lower Hill Barton Rd *EX1* 25 F2
Lower King's Av *EXN* EX4 ....16 A5
Lower La *TOP/EXT* EX3 ....44 A2
Lower Marlpits Hl *HON* EX14 ....5 F4
Lower Northcote Rd *HON* EX14 .....5 H1
Lower St German's Rd *EXN* EX4 ...15 H5
Lower Shapter St *TOP/EXT* EX3 ...43 F2
Lower Summerlands *EX1* 3 F2
Lower Wy *SID* EX10 ....29 E4
Lower Wear Rd *EXS* EX2 ....35 E3
Lower Wheathill *SID* EX10 ....30 D5
Lucas Av *EXN* EX4 ....16 A5

Lucky La *EXS* EX2 ....2 C5
Ludwell La *EXS* EX2 ....25 E5
Lumley Cl *REXSW* EX6 ....54 B1
Lustleigh Cl *EX1* 33 H3
Lymeborne Av *EX1* 24 D2
Lymebourne Av *SID* EX10 ....38 D2
Lymebourne La *SID* EX10 ....38 D2
Lymebourne Pk *SID* EX10 ....38 D2
Lynch Head *OTT* EX11 ....28 A3
Lyncombe Cl *EXN* EX4 ....16 B4
Lyndhurst Rd *EXM* EX8 ....56 B4
    EXS EX2 ....3 G5
Lynwood Av *EXN* EX4 ....23 F3

M

Macauley Cl *HON* EX14 ....5 F2
Madagascar Cl *EXM* EX8 ....57 F4
Madeira Vls *EXM* EX8 ....56 B5
Madison Av *EX1* 24 D2
Maer La *EXM* EX8 ....62 D2
Maer Rd *EXM* EX8 ....62 D2
Maer V *EXM* EX8 ....62 D1
Magdalen Gdns *EXS* EX2 * 3 G4
Magdalen Rd *EXS* EX2 ....3 F4
Magdalen St *EXS* EX2 ....2 D4
Magnolia Av *EXM* EX8 ....57 F4
    EXS EX2 ....24 D5
Magpie Crs *EXS* EX2 ....22 C4
Main Rd *EX1* 17 H3
Malden Cl *SID* EX10 ....38 D1
Malden La *SID* EX10 ....30 D5
Malden Rd *SID* EX10 ....30 D5
Mallard Rd *EXS* EX2 ....25 H3
Mallison Cl *EXN* EX4 ....15 E5
Mallocks Cl *SID* EX10 ....29 E1
Malt Fld *EXM* EX8 ....50 D4
Malvern Gdns *EXS* EX2 ....24 D4
Malvern Rd *SID* EX10 ....38 C2
Mamhead Rd *EXS* EX2 ....25 F4
Mamhead Vw *EXM* EX8 ....61 H1
Manaton Cl *EXS* EX2 ....33 H3
Manchester Rd *EXM* EX8 ....62 A1
Manchester St *EXM* EX8 ....56 A5
Mandrake Cl *EXS* EX2 ....33 G2
Mandrake Rd *EXS* EX2 ....33 F2
Manley Cl *REXNE* EX5 ....10 A2
Manor Cl *SID* EX10 ....38 C3
Manor Crs *HON* EX14 ....4 B5
Manor Pk *REXNE* EX5 ....26 B5
Manor Rd *EXS* EX2 ....23 F3
    SID EX10 ....38 C3
Mansfield Rd *EXN* EX4 ....16 B5
Mansfield Ter *BUD* EX9 ....59 G2
Manstone Av *SID* EX10 ....38 C1
Manstone Cl *SID* EX10 ....30 D5
Manstone La *SID* EX10 ....38 D1
Manstone Md *SID* EX10 ....30 D5
Manston Rd *EX1* 24 C1
Manston Ter *EXS* EX2 ....3 H4
Manstree Rd *EXS* EX2 ....40 A2
Maple Cl *HON* EX14 ....4 B5
Maple Dr *EXM* EX8 ....57 E1
Maple Ms *BUD* EX9 * 59 G2
Maple Rd *EXN* EX4 ....23 E3
    REXNE EX5 ....9 G4
Marcom Cl *EXM* EX8 ....57 E1
Marcus Rd *EXM* EX8 ....56 D3
Mardon Hl *EXN* EX4 ....15 G4
Margaret Rd *EXN* EX4 ....16 B4
Marine Pde *BUD* EX9 ....59 G4
Marine Wy *EXM* EX8 ....56 B5
The Marino *SID* EX10 ....38 D3
Marions Wy *EXM* EX8 ....57 E2
Maristow Av *EXM* EX8 ....56 C2
Marker Wy *HON* EX14 ....5 E3
Market St *EXM* EX8 ....62 B1
    EXN EX4 ....2 C3
Markham La *EXS* EX2 ....32 C4
Marlborough Cl *EXM* EX8 ....57 F2
Marlborough Dr *EXS* EX2 ....25 G3
Marlborough Rd *EXS* EX2 ....3 F5
The Marles *EXM* EX8 ....56 C2
Marley Dr *EXM* EX8 ....51 H4
Marley Rd *EXM* EX8 ....56 D2
Marlpits La *HON* EX14 ....5 E3
Marlpool Hl *EXM* EX8 ....56 C5
Marpool Crs *EXM* EX8 ....56 D4
Marpool Hl *EXM* EX8 ....56 D4
Marsh Barton Rd *EXS* EX2 ....23 G5
Marsh Green La *REXNE* EX5 ....20 B4
Marsh Green Rd East *EXS* EX2 ....33 H1
Marsh Green Rd North *EXS* EX2 ..33 H1
Marsh Green Rd West *EXS* EX2 ...33 G1
Marsh La *TOP/EXT* EX3 ....36 C5
Martins Rd *EXM* EX8 ....57 F2
Mary Arches St *EXN* EX4 ....2 A3

Maryfield Av *EXN* EX4 ....16 A5
Marypole Rd *EXN* EX4 ....16 C4
Masefield Rd *EXN* EX4 ....17 F5
Masey Rd *EXM* EX8 ....57 E4
Masterson St *EXS* EX2 ....3 J7
Matford Av *EXS* EX2 ....23 H5
Matford La *EXS* EX2 ....2 E6
Matford Ms *EXS* EX2 * 34 B4
Matford Park Rd *EXS* EX2 ....33 H3
Mathews Cl *HON* EX14 ....4 D4
Matthews Ct *EXN* EX4 ....17 G3
Maunder's Hl *BUD* EX9 ....53 G2
Mayfield Dr *EXM* EX8 ....62 D1
Mayfield Rd *EXN* EX4 ....17 H4
    EXS EX2 ....24 D3
Mayflower Av *EXN* EX4 ....16 A3
May St *EXN* EX4 ....16 A5
Meadow Crs *EXN* EX4 ....63 H1
Meadow Dr *SID* EX10 ....28 D5
Meadow Rd *BUD* EX9 ....59 E4
Meadows Crs *HON* EX14 ....5 E3
Meadow St *EXM* EX8 ....56 B5
Meadow Vw *EXM* EX8 * 50 D4
Meadow View Cl *SID* EX10 ....39 E3
Meadowview Rd *EXS* EX2 ....5 F2
Meadow Wy *EXS* EX2 ....3 K5
Mead View Rd *HON* EX14 ....5 E3
Meadway *SID* EX10 ....38 D2
The Mede *EXN* EX4 ....17 E5
    TOP/EXT EX3 ....43 E1
Medieval Br *EXN* EX4 ....2 A5
Medley Ct *EXN* EX4 ....14 D5
Meeting La *EXM* EX8 ....48 D5
Meeting St *EXM* EX8 ....56 B5
Melbourne Pl *EXS* EX2 ....2 D5
Melbourne St *EXS* EX2 ....2 D6
Membury Cl *EX1* * 25 G2
Mercer Cl *EXS* EX2 * 34 D1
Merlin Crs *EXN* EX4 ....16 D4
Mermaid Yd *EX1* 2 B4
Merrion Av *EXM* EX8 ....63 E1
Merrivale Rd *EXN* EX4 ....23 E4
Metcombe Ri *OTT* EX11 ....28 D1
Michigan Wy *EXN* EX4 ....15 H3
Middle St *BUD* EX9 ....52 D3
Middletown La *BUD* EX9 ....52 D3
Middlewood *REXSW* EX6 ....60 D2
Midway *EXM* EX8 ....57 F4
Midway Cl *EXS* EX2 ....33 F2
Milbury Cl *REXSW* EX6 ....42 A1
Milbury La *REXSW* EX6 ....42 B2
Mildmay Cl *EXN* EX4 ....23 E1
Mile Gdns *EXN* EX4 ....16 C3
Mile La *EX1* 16 D4
Milford Av *SID* EX10 ....30 D4
Milford Rd *SID* EX10 ....38 D4
Millbrook La *EXS* EX2 ....34 C1
Milldale Crs *HON* EX14 ....4 D3
Miller Cl *EXS* EX2 ....25 F4
Millers Wy *HON* EX14 ....4 D3
Miller Wy *REXSW* EX6 ....41 H1
Milletts Cl *REXSW* EX6 ....42 A1
Millhead Rd *HON* EX14 ....4 B4
Mill La *EX1* 18 D4
    EXS EX2 ....33 G2
    OTT EX11 ....7 G4
    TOP/EXT EX3 ....44 B4
Millmoor La *SID* EX10 ....28 D5
Millmoor V *SID* EX10 ....28 D5
Mill Rd *EXS* EX2 ....34 C2
Millside *EXS* EX2 ....2 E7
Mill Stream Ct *OTT* EX11 ....12 C5
Mill St *HON* EX14 ....4 D5
    OTT EX11 ....12 C5
    SID EX10 ....38 D4
Milltown La *SID* EX10 ....39 E2
Milton Cl *EXM* EX8 ....51 G5
Milton Rd *EXS* EX2 ....24 C5
Mincinglake Rd *EXN* EX4 ....16 C4
Minifie Rd *HON* EX14 ....4 D2
The Mint *EXN* EX4 * 2 B4
Mirey La *REXNE* EX5 ....45 F3
Mitre La *EXN* EX4 ....2 A3
Modred Cl *EXN* EX4 ....16 D4
Monitor Cl *EXS* EX2 ....2 B7
Monkerton Cl *EX1* 17 H5
Monkerton Dr *EX1* 17 H5
Monk's Rd *EXN* EX4 ....24 B1
Monkswell Rd *EXN* EX4 ....16 B5
Monkton Rd *HON* EX14 ....5 F2
Monmouth Av *TOP/EXT* EX3 ....43 F1
Monmouth Hl *TOP/EXT* EX3 ....43 F2
Monmouth St *TOP/EXT* EX3 ....43 F2
Monmouth Wy *HON* EX14 ....5 F3

Montague Ri EXN EX4 23 H1
Mont Le Grand EX EX1 3 H3
Montpellier Rd EXM EX8 56 B5
Moon Hill Cl EXS EX2 33 H3
Moonridge EXS EX2 35 F4
Moorcourt Cl SID EX10 38 B5
Mooredge La REXNE EX5 9 E1
Moorfield Cl EXM EX8 56 D4
Moorfield Rd EXM EX8 56 D4
Moorhaven BUD EX9 59 E2
Moorlands OTT EX11 21 F3
Moorlands Rd BUD EX9 58 C3
Moorland Wy EXN EX4 14 D5
Moor La BUD EX9 59 E2
EXN EX4 8 C3
EXS EX2 25 H2
SID EX10 28 C3
Moormead BUD EX9 59 E3
Moor Pk EXM EX8 * 62 D1
HON EX14 4 D5
Moorview Cl EXN EX4 16 A4
Moor View Cl SID EX10 38 B1
Morley Rd EXN EX4 16 B5
Mortimer Ct EXS EX2 * 34 D1
Morton Crs EXM EX8 62 A1
Morton Crescent Ms EXM EX8 62 A1
Morton Rd EXM EX8 62 A1
Morven Dr EXM EX8 56 B2
Mosshayne La EX EX1 18 C2
Mossop Cl OTT EX11 12 D5
Mountain Cl EXM EX8 57 G4
Mountbatten Cl EXM EX8 57 E2
Mount Cl HON EX14 4 D3
Mount Dinham EXN EX4 * 23 F2
Mount Pleasant Av EXM EX8 56 C1
Mount Pleasant Rd EXN EX4 16 B5
Mount Radford Crs EXS EX2 2 E5
Mount Ri REXSW EX6 47 E2
Mount Vw HON EX14 6 D1
Mount Wear Sq EXS EX2 35 E3
Mowbray Av EXN EX4 2 D1
Mudbank La EXM EX8 56 B4
Mulberry Cl EX EX1 25 E2
Musgrave Rw EXN EX4 2 C2
Mushroom Rd REXNE EX5 27 H5
Myrtle Cl EXS EX2 33 G2
Myrtle Rd EXN EX4 22 D4
Myrtle Rw EXM EX8 62 B1

N

Nadder La EXN EX4 14 A5
Nadder Park Rd EXN EX4 22 C3
Nasmith Cl EXM EX8 57 E3
Nelson Cl TOP/EXT EX3 43 E1
Nelson Dr EXM EX8 57 F4
Nelson Rd EXN EX4 23 F4
Nethercott Pl EX EX1 3 K4
New Bridge St EXN EX4 2 A5
Newcombe St EX EX1 3 K3
Newcombe Ter EX EX1 * 3 K3
Newcourt Rd TOP/EXT EX3 35 H4
Newfoundland Cl EXN EX4 16 A3
Newhayes Cl EXS EX2 33 F1
Newlands HON EX14 5 E2
Newlands Av EXM EX8 57 E3
Newlands Cl EXS EX2 33 F1
SID EX10 30 D5
Newlands Rd SID EX10 30 D5
New La OTT EX11 13 E4
Newman Ct EXN EX4 22 D3
Newman Rd EXN EX4 23 E3
New North Rd EXM EX8 56 B5
EXN EX4 2 B1
Newport Rd EXS EX2 35 F4
New Rd REXNE EX5 20 D3
REXSW EX6 54 D4
New St EXM EX8 56 B5
HON EX14 5 E2
OTT EX11 13 E4
SID EX10 38 D5
Newtown SID EX10 38 D4
Newtown Cl EX EX1 * 3 F2
New Valley Rd EXN EX4 23 E1
Nicholas Rd EX EX1 24 D2
Nichols Wy EXN EX4 24 B1
Nightingale Wk EXS EX2 22 C5
Norman Cl EXM EX8 57 E2
Norman Crs BUD EX9 59 F2
Normandy Cl EXM EX8 57 F3
Normandy Rd EX EX1 3 K3
Norman Ms EXS EX2 25 G4
Norman Pl EXS EX2 25 G4
North Av EX EX1 3 H2
Northbrook Cl EXN EX4 16 D4
Northcote Hl HON EX14 5 H1
Northcote La HON EX14 4 D2
Northcote Rd HON EX14 5 G1
Northernhay Pl EXN EX4 2 C2
Northernhay Sq EXN EX4 2 B2
Northernhay St EXN EX4 2 B3
North Lawn Ct EX EX1 3 K2
Northleigh Hill Rd HON EX14 5 G5
North Park Rd EXN EX4 15 G4
North St EX EX1 3 K3
EXM EX8 56 B5
EXN EX4 2 B3
OTT EX11 13 E4
TOP/EXT EX3 43 F2
Northview Rd BUD EX9 59 E4
Norwich Cl EXM EX8 51 H5
Norwich Rd EXN EX4 22 D2
Norwood Av EXS EX2 2 E7
Nurseries Cl TOP/EXT EX3 35 H5
TOP/EXT EX3 44 A5
Nursery Cl EXM EX8 56 D4
Nursery Ms EXM EX8 56 D4
Nutbrook EXM EX8 56 C3
Nutwell Rd EXM EX8 50 C3

O

Oak Cl EX EX1 * 3 K4
EXN EX4 17 H4
EXS EX2 33 F5
OTT EX11 12 D5
REXSW EX6 42 A2
Oakfield Rd EXN EX4 23 F3
Oakfield St EX EX1 3 J4
Oakhayes Rd REXNE EX5 45 F3
Oak Hl BUD EX9 52 D4
Oaklea HON EX14 4 D2
Oakleigh Rd EXM EX8 56 C5
Oakley Cl EX EX1 17 H4
Oakridge EXS EX2 33 F3
Oak Rd EXN EX4 23 E4
REXNE EX5 20 D5
Oaktree Cl EXM EX8 56 C1
REXNE EX5 9 G4
Oak Vw HON EX14 4 C5
Oakwood Ri EXM EX8 57 F1
Oberon Rd EX EX1 25 H1
Oilmill La REXNE EX5 36 D1
Okehampton Pl EXN EX4 23 F3
Okehampton Rd EXN EX4 23 E3
Okehampton St EXN EX4 23 F3
Old Abbey Ct EXS EX2 24 B5
Old Bakery Cl EXN EX4 23 E1
Old Bystock Dr EXM EX8 57 F1
Old Coach Rd REXNE EX5 9 F4
Old Dawlish Rd REXSW EX6 40 D4
Old Ebford La TOP/EXT EX3 44 A2
Old Elm Rd HON EX14 4 B4
Oldfields EXM EX8 62 D1
Old Fore St SID EX10 38 D5
Old Ide La EXS EX2 32 D1
Old Market Cl EXS EX2 * 23 G5
Old Matford La REXSW EX6 41 G1
Old Mill Cl EXS EX2 2 E7
Old Park Rd EXN EX4 2 D1
Old Pavilion Cl EXS EX2 25 F4
Old Pinn La EX EX1 17 H5
Old Rydon Cl EXS EX2 35 H1
Old Rydon La EXS EX2 35 G2
Old Rydon Ley EXS EX2 35 G1
The Old Saddlery HON EX14 5 F3
Old's Vw EXN EX4 23 F1
Old Tiverton Rd EXN EX4 24 A1
Old Vicarage Cl EXS EX2 32 C2
Old Vicarage Rd EXS EX2 23 F4
The Old Vicarage SID EX10 38 B5
Olive Gdns DAW EX7 61 E5
Olive Gv DAW EX7 61 E5
Orchard Cl BUD EX9 52 D4
EX EX1 18 A4
EXM EX8 50 C4
OTT EX11 13 E5
REXNE EX5 45 G3
SID EX10 28 B5
SID EX10 31 E5
SID EX10 38 B5
Orchard Dr BUD EX9 53 G2
Orchard Gdns EXN EX4 23 E4
REXNE EX5 9 G4
Orchard Hl EXS EX2 22 D5
Orchard La REXSW EX6 60 D3
Orchardside SID EX10 38 D1
The Orchard SID EX10 29 E1
Orchard Vw EX EX1 * 3 K4
Orchard Wy HON EX14 5 F2
REXSW EX6 54 A1
TOP/EXT EX3 43 E1
Oriole Dr EXN EX4 16 A4
Orwell Garth EXN EX4 17 F4
Osprey Rd EXS EX2 26 A2
Otter Cl OTT EX11 21 F4
Otter Ct BUD EX9 59 H3
Otter Reach BUD EX9 * 59 G2
SID EX10 28 D5
Ottervale Rd BUD EX9 59 H3
Ottery La SID EX10 31 E3
Ottery Moor La HON EX14 4 C2
Ottery St BUD EX9 53 G2
Outer Ting Tong BUD EX9 58 A1
Oxford Rd EXN EX4 2 E1
Oxford St EXS EX2 23 F4

P

Packhorse Cl SID EX10 31 F5
The Paddocks REXNE EX5 10 B4
Painters Ct EXS EX2 2 B6
Palace Ga EX EX1 2 C4
Pale Gate Cl HON EX14 5 E1
Palm Cl EXM EX8 57 E1
Palm Ct DAW EX7 60 D5
Palmer Ms BUD EX9 * 59 F4
Palmer's La REXNE EX5 20 B3
Palmerston Dr EXN EX4 22 D1
Pamela Rd EXN EX4 24 C1
Pankhurst Cl EXM EX8 57 F5
The Panney EXN EX4 24 D1
Parade EXM EX8 56 B5
Paris St EXN EX4 2 D2
Paris Street Ar EXN EX4 * 2 D2
Park Cl REXNE EX5 45 G4
Park Ct HON EX14 4 B4
Parkers Cross La EX EX1 18 A3
Parker's Rd REXSW EX6 54 D4
Parkfield Rd TOP/EXT EX3 43 F1
Parkhouse Rd EXS EX2 23 E5
Parkland Dr EXS EX2 25 F5
Park La BUD EX9 53 G3
EXM EX8 56 B4
EXN EX4 17 H2
Park Pl EX EX1 3 J3
EXS EX2 3 F5
Park Rd EX EX1 3 H1
EXM EX8 56 B4
Parkside Crs EX EX1 18 A2
Parkside Dr EXM EX8 57 E2
Parkside Rd EX EX1 18 A2
Park Vw EXM EX8 * 51 E4
Parkway EXS EX2 23 E5
Park Wy EXM EX8 56 D4
REXNE EX5 45 G4
Parr Cl EX EX1 * 3 F1
Parr St EX EX1 3 F1
Parsonage Cross REXNE EX5 45 G3
Parsonage La HON EX14 5 F3
Parsonage Wy REXNE EX5 45 G3
Parson Cl EXM EX8 56 D2
Parthia Pl EXM EX8 57 F3
Partridge Rd EXM EX8 56 D2
Pathwhorlands SID EX10 38 C2
Patricia Cl EXN EX4 15 H3
Patteson Cl OTT EX11 7 G5
Patteson Dr OTT EX11 13 E4
Paul St EXN EX4 2 B2
Pauntley Gdn SID EX10 38 B5
Pavilion Pl EXS EX2 2 D4
Paynes Ct EXN EX4 * 17 E5
Peacock Pl REXSW EX6 54 D4
Peartree Cl REXSW EX6 54 A1
Peaslands Rd SID EX10 38 C3
Peel Rw EXN EX4 17 F5
Pellinore Rd EXN EX4 16 D4
Pendragon Rd EXN EX4 16 C3
Penhayes Cl REXSW EX6 54 A1
Penhayes Rd REXSW EX6 54 B1
Peninsula Pk EXS EX2 * 25 F4
Penlee BUD EX9 59 E4
Penleonard Cl EXS EX2 3 G5
Pennant House EXM EX8 61 H1
Pennsylvania Cl EXN EX4 16 A5
Pennsylvania Crs EXN EX4 15 H5
Pennsylvania Pk EXN EX4 16 A4
Pennsylvania Rd EXN EX4 15 H5
Penny Cl REXSW EX6 42 A2
Perceval Rd EXN EX4 16 D3
Percy Rd EXS EX2 23 G5
Perriam's Pl BUD EX9 59 F4
Perridge Cl EXS EX2 22 C5
Perriman's Rw EXM EX8 * 56 B5
Perry Rd EXN EX4 15 G5
Perrys Gdns OTT EX11 21 F4
Perth Cl EXN EX4 16 B3
Peryam Crs EXS EX2 24 D4
Peterborough Rd EXN EX4 22 D1
Phear Av EXM EX8 56 C5
Philip Rd EXN EX4 16 C5
Phillipps Av EXM EX8 56 C3
Phillips Sq HON EX14 4 D2
Piazza Terracina EXS EX2 * 2 C6
Pier Head EXM EX8 61 H1
Pilton La EXN EX4 17 G5
Pinaster Cl HON EX14 5 G3
Pinbrook Rd EXN EX4 17 G4
Pinces Gdns EXS EX2 23 F5
Pinces Rd EXS EX2 23 F5
Pine Av EXN EX4 23 E1
Pine Gdns HON EX14 5 F2
Pine Gv HON EX14 5 F2
Pine Park Rd HON EX14 5 F3
Pineridge Cl EXN EX4 23 E4
Pines Rd EXM EX8 56 D1
The Pines EXN EX4 23 E1
HON EX14 5 F3
Pine Tree Cl DAW EX7 61 E5
Pine View Cl EXM EX8 57 G2
Pinhoe Rd EX EX1 17 H5
EXN EX4 17 F5
Pinnbridge Ct EX EX1 * 17 H5
Pinncourt La EXN EX4 18 A3
Pinn Hl EX EX1 18 A3
Pinn La EX EX1 25 H1
Pinn Valley Rd EX EX1 18 A4
Pinwood La EXN EX4 17 E3
Pinwood Meadow Dr EXN EX4 17 E3
Pippin Cl EX EX1 25 F2
Piscombe La BUD EX9 53 H3
Pitham La OTT EX11 13 E1
Pitt Hl REXSW EX6 54 A1
Plassey Cl EXN EX4 16 A3
Playmoor Dr EX EX1 17 H4
Plume of Feathers Cl OTT EX11 13 E4
Plumtree Dr EXS EX2 25 E4
Plumtree La REXNE EX5 10 B4
Pocombe Br EXS EX2 22 C5
Pocombe Hl EXS EX2 22 C5
Point Ter EXM EX8 61 H1
Polehouse La EXS EX2 32 D2
Polsloe Rd EX EX1 3 H2
Poltimore Sq EXN EX4 2 D1
Poplar DAW EX7 60 D5
Poplar Cl EXM EX8 57 E1
EXS EX2 23 F5
The Poplars EXN EX4 17 H3
Poppy Cl EXN EX4 14 C5
Porter's La EXM EX8 50 C1
Portland Av EXM EX8 62 C1
Portland St EX EX1 3 F2
Port Mer Cl EXM EX8 57 F1
Port Rd DAW EX7 60 B3
Post Office St EX EX1 2 D3
Pottery Cl HON EX14 5 F2
Pottles Cl REXSW EX6 42 A3
Pound Cl EXM EX8 56 D3
TOP/EXT EX3 35 H5
Pound La EXM EX8 56 C2
REXNE EX5 45 G2
TOP/EXT EX3 35 H5
Poundsland REXNE EX5 9 F4
Pound St EXM EX8 62 B1
Powderham Cl TOP/EXT EX3 35 H5
Powderham Crs EXN EX4 24 A1
Powderham Rd EXS EX2 23 E4
Powhay Mills EXN EX4 * 23 F3
Powlesland Rd EXS EX2 33 G2
Premier Pl EXS EX2 3 F5
Prescot Rd EXN EX4 22 D3
Preston St EX EX1 2 B4
Pretoria Rd EX EX1 3 H1
Priddis Cl EXM EX8 56 D1
Pridhams Wy REXSW EX6 42 A2
Priestley Av EXN EX4 17 E5
Primley Gdns SID EX10 39 E1
Primley Md SID EX10 38 D1
Primley Paddock SID EX10 38 D1
Primley Rd SID EX10 39 E1
Primrose Lawn EXN EX4 14 C5
Prince Charles Cl EXM EX8 57 F3
Prince Charles Rd EXN EX4 16 B5
Prince of Wales Dr EXM EX8 57 F3
Prince of Wales Rd EXN EX4 15 G5
Prince's St West EXS EX2 23 F4
Princesshay EXN EX4 2 C3
Princesshay La EX EX1 2 D2
Prince's Sq EXS EX2 23 F5
Princes St EXM EX8 56 B5
Prince's St East EXS EX2 23 F5
Prince's St North EXS EX2 23 F4
Prince's St South EXS EX2 23 F5
Priory Cl BUD EX9 52 D3
Priory Gdns EXN EX4 * 2 A4
Priory Rd EXN EX4 16 B5
Prospect Gdns EXN EX4 24 B1
Prospect Pk EXN EX4 16 A5
Prospect Pl EXN EX4 23 F4
Puckridge Rd EXN EX4 17 G3

Puffin Wy EXS EX2....22 C5
Pulling Rd EXN EX4....17 G3
Pulpit Wk EXS EX2....33 H4
Purcell Cl EXS EX2....25 F3
Pye Cnr REXSW EX6....40 D4
Pynes Cl BUD EX9....52 D3
Pynes Hl EXS EX2....35 E1
Pytte Gdns TOP/EXT EX3....36 D4

Q

The Quadrangle EXN EX4....15 H5
The Quadrant EXS EX2 *....2 E5
The Quarries EXN EX4....22 C4
Quarry La EXS EX2....25 F3
Quarry Park Rd EXS EX2....25 F4
Quay La EX EX1....2 B5
The Quay EXS EX2....2 B5
Queen's Crs EXN EX4....2 D1
Queen's Dr EXM EX8....62 C2
The Queen's Dr EXN EX4....15 G5
Queensland Dr EXM EX8....16 B3
Queen's Rd BUD EX9....59 E4
Queens EXS EX2....23 F5
Queens Ter EXN EX4....2 A1
Queen St BUD EX9....59 F4
  EXM EX8....62 B1
  EXN EX4....2 A1
  HON EX14....5 E2
Questant La SID EX10....39 E2
Quintet EX EX1....25 F3

R

Rackclose La EXN EX4....2 A4
Rack St EX EX1....2 B4
Raddenstile La EXM EX8....62 C1
Radford Rd EXS EX2....2 D5
Radnor Pl EX EX1....2 E4
Radway SID EX10....38 D4
Ragg La BUD EX9....59 F4
Raglans EXS EX2....33 H3
Raleigh Cl SID EX10....38 D1
Raleigh Rd BUD EX9....59 G3
  EXM EX8....62 B1
  EXS EX2....3 F4
  OTT EX11....13 E4
Rance Dr EXM EX8....57 F1
Raven Cl EXN EX4....15 H4
Rayners REXSW EX6....40 C5
Read Cl EXM EX8....56 D3
Rectory Dr REXNE EX5....10 A2
Rectory Dr EXS EX2....33 G3
Red Cow Village EXN EX4 *....23 F1
Reddaway Dr REXSW EX6....41 H1
Redhills BUD EX9....59 F4
  EXN EX4....22 C2
Redhills Cl EXN EX4....22 D2
Redlands Cl EXN EX4....16 D5
Red Lion La EX EX1....2 E1
Redvers Rd EXN EX4....23 F3
Redwood Cl EXM EX8....57 E1
  HON EX14....4 B4
Redwood Rd SID EX10....38 D3
Regency Crs EXM EX8....62 C1
Regency Ga SID EX10....39 E3
Regents Ga EXM EX8....62 C1
Regent's Pk EX EX1....3 H2
Regent Sq EX EX1....3 K4
Regent St EXS EX2....23 F5
Reme Dr HON EX14....4 B4
Rennes Dr EXN EX4....15 H4
Retail Park Cl EXS EX2....23 G5
The Retreat Dr TOP/EXT EX3....35 G5
Retreat Rd TOP/EXT EX3....43 E1
Rews Meadow EX EX1....17 H4
Rews Park Dr EX EX1....18 A4
Rexona Cl EX EX1....33 F1
Reynolds Cl EXN EX4....17 G4
Ribston Av EX EX1....25 F2
Rices Ms EXS EX2....23 F5
Richards Cl EXM EX8....57 E2
Richmond Rd EXM EX8....57 F1
  EXN EX4....2 A2
Ridgeway EXN EX4....15 F2
  HON EX14....4 C4
  OTT EX11....13 E4
Ridge Wy REXSW EX6....54 B2
Ridgeway SID EX10....31 F1
Ridgeway Cl SID EX10....31 F1
Ridgeway Gdns OTT EX11....13 E4
Ridgeway Md SID EX10....38 B1
The Ridings TOP/EXT EX3....44 B2
Rifford Rd EXS EX2....25 E4
Rill La BUD EX9....59 G4

Ringswell Av EX EX1....25 F2
River Front TOP/EXT EX3....43 H4
Rivermead Av EXM EX8....56 B2
River Mdw EXS EX2....23 H5
Rivermead Rd EXS EX2....24 A5
Riverside Cl HON EX14....4 D2
Riverside Rd SID EX10....38 D4
  TOP/EXT EX3....35 G5
Riverside Vw OTT EX11....12 D5
Rivers Wk EXS EX2....35 F4
Riverview Dr EXN EX4....15 E5
Roberts Rd EXS EX2....2 B5
Robert Wy SID EX10....28 D5
Roche Gdn EXS EX2....34 D3
Rodney Cl EXM EX8....57 H5
Rolle Rd BUD EX9....59 F4
  EXM EX8....62 B1
Rollestone Crs EXM EX8....16 B3
Rolle St EXM EX8....62 B1
Rolle Vls EXM EX8....62 B1
Roman Rd HON EX14....5 G1
Roman Wy HON EX14....5 G1
Romsey Dr EXS EX2....3 G5
Rookwood Cl HON EX14....4 D2
Ropers Ct BUD EX9....53 G2
Roper's La BUD EX9....53 G2
Ropewalk House EXM EX8....61 H1
Rosebank Crs EXN EX4....16 A4
Rosebarn Av EXN EX4....16 A4
Rosebarn La EXN EX4....16 A3
Rosebery Rd EXM EX8....16 B5
  EXN EX4....16 B5
Roseland Av EXN EX4....24 D2
Roseland Crs EX EX1....24 D2
Roseland Dr EX EX1....3 K4
Roselands SID EX10....38 C4
Rosemary St EXS EX2....23 E3
Rosemont Ct EXS EX2....33 G2
The Rosemullion BUD EX9 *....59 F4
Roseway EXM EX8....57 F4
Rosewell Cl HON EX14....5 F1
Rosewood Crs REXNE EX5....37 E1
Rosewood Ter EXN EX4....16 A5
Ross Cl EX EX1....18 A4
Rougemont Ct REXSW EX6 *....41 H2
Roundball Cl HON EX14....5 E4
Roundhill Cl EXN EX4....15 E2
Roundhouse La EXM EX8....56 C2
Roundtable Meet EXN EX4....16 D2
Rowan Cl HON EX14....4 D4
Rowan Wy EXN EX4....23 E1
Rowcroft Cl HON EX14....4 D4
Rowhorne Rd EXN EX4....14 B5
Rowlstone Cl EXM EX8....56 D1
The Royal EXM EX8....56 C5
Royal Cl EXS EX2....33 G4
Royal Crs EXS EX2....25 G5
Royal Wy REXSW EX6....55 E4
Rugby Rd EXN EX4....23 E1
Rushforth Pl EXN EX4....14 D5
Russell Dr BUD EX9....52 D3
Russell St EX EX1....3 F2
  SID EX10....38 D5
Russell Ter EXN EX4 *....23 F1
Russell Wk EXS EX2....25 F5
Russell Wy EXS EX2....35 G1
Russet Av EX EX1....25 F5
Rutherford St EXS EX2....24 D4
Rydon La EXS EX2....35 E2
  TOP/EXT EX3....44 B4
Rydon Pk EXS EX2 *....25 G4
Ryll Cl EXM EX8....56 B5
Ryll Court Dr EXM EX8....56 C5
Ryll Gv EXM EX8....56 C5

S

Sadler Cl EXM EX8....57 F4
Sailmakers Ct EXM EX8....61 H1
St Andrew's Cl REXSW EX6....47 E2
St Andrew's Rd EXM EX8....62 A1
  EXN EX4....15 E4
St Annes REXSW EX6....54 A1
St Anne's Rd EX EX1....24 B1
St Anthony's Cl OTT EX11....13 E4
St Bernard's Cl EXS EX2....2 E7
St Briac Wy EXM EX8....57 F1
St Budeaux Cl OTT EX11....13 E5
St Cyres Rd HON EX14....4 D2
St Davids EXN EX4 *....23 F1
St David's Hl EXN EX4....2 A2
St Davids Pl EXN EX4 *....23 F1
St Davids Ter EXN EX4 *....2 A2
St German's Rd EXN EX4....15 H5

St Hill Cl EXS EX2....33 F1
St Ida's Cl EXS EX2....32 C2
St James Cl EXN EX4....24 A1
St James' Rd EXN EX4....24 A1
St James Ter EXN EX4 *....24 A1
St John's Rd EX EX1....24 B1
  EXM EX8....57 F3
St Katherines Rd EXN EX4....16 D5
St Lawrence Crs EX EX1....25 F2
St Leonard's Av EXS EX2....2 D6
St Leonard's Pl EXS EX2....2 E5
St Leonard's Rd EXS EX2....2 E5
St Leonards Rd HON EX14....4 C3
St Loyes EXS EX2....24 D3
St Loye's Ter EXS EX2....24 D4
St Malo Cl EXM EX8....57 F1
St Margarets Ter
  TOP/EXT EX3 *....43 F1
St Margaret's Vw EXM EX8....57 H5
St Marks Av EXN EX4....24 C1
St Mark's Rd HON EX14....4 C4
St Martins Cl SID EX10....38 D2
St Marys Pk OTT EX11....13 F5
St Mary Steps Ter EX EX1 *....2 B4
St Mathews Wk EX EX1 *....3 F2
St Matthews Cl EXS EX2....3 G2
St Michaels Cl BUD EX9....53 G2
St Michael's Cl EXS EX2....33 G2
  REXNE EX5....19 E5
St Michael's Hl REXNE EX5....19 E5
St Olave's Cl EXS EX2....2 B4
St Paul's Rd HON EX14....4 C4
St Peters Mt EXN EX4....22 C2
St Petrocks Cl EXS EX2....3 F5
St Saviours Rd OTT EX11....12 D5
St Sevan Wy EX EX1....57 F1
St Sidwell's Av EXN EX4....24 A1
St Thomas Ct EXN EX4....23 F4
Salcombe Hill Cl SID EX10....38 D4
Salcombe Hill Rd SID EX10....39 E4
Salcombe Rd SID EX10....38 D4
Salem Pl EX EX1 *....3 F1
Salisbury Rd EXM EX8....56 B5
  EXN EX4....16 B5
Salmonpool La EXS EX2....24 B5
Salterne Mdw BUD EX9....59 F2
Salters Meadow SID EX10....38 D3
Salter's Rd EXS EX2....24 D4
Salterton Ct EXM EX8....57 G4
Salterton Rd EXM EX8....62 C1
Salting Hl BUD EX9....59 H4
Saltways La SID EX10....30 A4
Salutary Mt EX EX1 *....3 J4
Sampson's Hl EXS EX2....40 B3
Sampsons La EX EX1....3 H1
Sanders Cl REXNE EX5....9 G4
Sanders Rd EXN EX4....17 H4
Sandfords REXSW EX6....46 C1
Sandford Wk EXS EX2....3 F2
Sandhill St OTT EX11....13 E4
Sandpiper DAW EX7....60 C5
Sandpiper Dr TOP/EXT EX3....44 A4
Sandpiper Gn EXS EX2....22 C4
Sandy La REXNE EX5....9 G5
Sannerville Wy REXSW EX6....34 D5
Sargent Cl EX EX1....25 F2
Sarlsdown Rd EXM EX8....56 D5
Savile Rd EXN EX4....23 E4
Savoy Hl EXN EX4....16 D3
Sawmill La BUD EX9....52 B2
Sawmills Wy HON EX14....5 E3
Saxon Av EXN EX4....22 D4
Saxon Rd EX EX1....3 K3
School Hl EXM EX8....50 C4
  REXSW EX6....61 E1
School La EXM EX8....56 D3
  EXS EX2....34 D2
  HON EX14....5 E1
  OTT EX11....21 F3
  REXNE EX5....9 F3
  SID EX10....28 D5
School Rd EXS EX2....23 F4
School St SID EX10....31 E4
Schooners Ct EXM EX8....61 H1
Scott Av EXS EX2....24 C5
Scott Dr EXM EX8....56 C2
Scratch Face La EXS EX2....32 B1
Seabrook Av EXS EX2....35 F4
Seabrook Ms EXS EX2....35 F4
Seafield Av EXM EX8....56 B2
Seafield La SID EX10....38 C5
Seafield Rd SID EX10....38 C4
Seaway La SID EX10....29 E2
Second Av EX EX1....3 J2
  EXS EX2....35 F4
Sedemuda Cl SID EX10....30 B5
Sedemuda Rd SID EX10....30 B5
Sedgeclaire Cl EX EX1....18 A4
Senate Wy EXM EX8....57 E3

Sentrys Orch REXSW EX6....42 B3
Sercombes Gdns REXSW EX6....56 D4
Seymore Cl EXM EX8....56 C2
Seymour Cl EXS EX2....56 C2
Seymour Ct EXM EX8....56 C2
Seymour Rd EXM EX8....56 C2
Shackleton Cl EXM EX8....56 C2
Shaftesbury Rd EXS EX2....23 F4
Shakespeare Rd EXS EX2....24 C5
Shakespeare Wy EXM EX8....61 H1
Sharps Ct EXM EX8....61 H1
Shelley Cl EXS EX2....33 F1
Shelly Reach EXM EX8....62 A1
Shelly Rd EXM EX8....61 H1
Shelton Pl EX EX1 *....3 K3
Shepherd's Hl EXS EX2....34 C2
Sheppard Rd EXN EX4....16 A3
Sheppard's Rw EXM EX8....56 B5
Sherbrook Cl BUD EX9....58 D4
Sherbrook Hl BUD EX9....58 D4
Shercroft Cl REXNE EX5....19 F3
Sheridan Rd EXN EX4....17 F3
Sherwell Cl DAW EX7....60 D5
Sherwood Cl EXS EX2....3 J5
Sherwood Ct EXS EX2....3 J5
Sherwood Dr EXM EX8....57 E1
Shiers Orch BUD EX9....52 A1
Shillingford La REXSW EX6....40 C2
Shillingford Rd EXS EX2....33 F4
Ship La REXNE EX5....19 E5
Shipley Rd HON EX14....5 F2
Shire Cl HON EX14....4 C3
Shirley Rd EXS EX2....51 H5
Shooting Marsh Stile EXS EX2....2 B6
Shortridge Cl HON EX14....5 E4
Shortwood Cl BUD EX9....59 G4
Shute Meadow St EXM EX8 *....56 B5
Shutes Md OTT EX11....13 E5
Shutterton Br DAW EX7....60 C5
Shutterton La DAW EX7....60 C5
Sidcliffe SID EX10....39 E2
Sidford Rd SID EX10....38 D1
Sidgard Rd SID EX10....38 D3
Sid La SID EX10....38 D3
Sidmount Gdns SID EX10....39 E2
Sidmouth Rd EXS EX2....25 F3
  HON EX14....4 C4
Sid Park Rd SID EX10....39 E2
Sid Rd SID EX10....39 E2
Sid Vale Cl SID EX10....31 E4
Sidwell St EXN EX4....2 C3
Sigford Rd EXS EX2....34 A3
The Signals HON EX14....6 D2
Silver Birch Cl EXS EX2....24 C5
Silverdale EXM EX8....57 F1
Silver La EX EX1....3 F1
The Silvers TOP/EXT EX3 *....36 A1
Silver St HON EX14....5 E2
  OTT EX11....12 D5
Silver Ter EXN EX4 *....2 A2
Silverton Rd EXS EX2....34 A3
Simey Cl EXN EX4....23 E1
Sivell Ms EX EX1....3 K4
Sivell Pl EXS EX2....3 K4
Skylark DAW EX7....60 D5
Slade Cl OTT EX11....13 F5
Slade Rd OTT EX11....13 F5
Sleap Hl BUD EX9....53 E2
Slewton Crs REXNE EX5....10 A1
Slittercombe La REXSW EX6....48 D5
Small La REXNE EX5....9 F3
Smith Field Rd EXS EX2....33 F3
Smiths Ct EXS EX2....2 B7
Smythen St EX EX1....2 B4
Snowdrop Cl HON EX14....4 C4
Snowdrop Ms EXN EX4....14 C5
Solar Crs EXN EX4....22 D4
Somerset Av EXN EX4....22 D4
Somerville Ct EXM EX8....57 E3
South Av EX EX1....3 H2
Southbrook Rd EXS EX2....34 D2
Southernhay East EX EX1....2 D4
Southernhay Gdns EX EX1....2 D4
Southernhay West EX EX1....2 D4
Southern Rd EXM EX8....56 B4
Southern Wd EXM EX8....57 F2
South Farm Rd BUD EX9....59 H1
South Ga EXS EX2....2 C5
South Lawn SID EX10....31 E5
South Lawn Ter EX EX1....3 K3
South Pde BUD EX9....59 G4
Southport Av EXN EX4....22 D3
South St EX EX1....2 B4
  EXM EX8....62 B1
South View Ter EXN EX4....16 A5
Southway SID EX10....39 E4
South West Coast Pth BUD EX9....59 E4
  EXM EX8....62 E3
  REXSW EX6....49 E1
  TOP/EXT EX3....43 E3
Sovereign Cl EXM EX8....57 F3

Sowden La EXM EX8 50 C5
Sowton La REXNE EX5 26 B2
Spencer Cl EXM EX8 57 F2
Spenser Av EXS EX2 24 C5
Spicer Rd EX EX1 3 F4
Spider's La EXM EX8 56 D1
Spindlewood Cl HON EX14 5 E5
Spinney Cl EXS EX2 25 F4
Spinning Pth EXN EX4 * 24 A1
Spitup La SID EX10 38 A1
Springfield Rd EXM EX8 56 C3
EXN EX4 16 A5
HON EX14 5 H3
Spring Gdns OTT EX11 13 E5
Spruce Cl EXM EX8 57 E1
EXN EX4 17 E3
The Square EXN EX4 15 E5
EXS EX2 25 G3
Staddon Cl EXN EX4 25 E1
Stadium Wy EXN EX4 24 A1
Staffick Cl REXSW EX6 54 B1
Stafford Rd EXN EX4 23 E3
Stanford Rd EXS EX2 25 F3
Stanhope Dr SID EX10 38 D2
Stanley Ms BUD EX9 * 59 F3
Stanley Sq TOP/EXT EX3 * 43 F2
Stanley Wk EXM EX8 51 H5
Stantyway Rd BUD EX9 53 H4
Stanwey EX EX1 24 D3
Staplake La REXSW EX6 54 D5
Staplake Rd REXSW EX6 54 D3
Star Barton La REXNE EX5 14 B1
Station Rd BUD EX9 59 F3
EX EX1 17 H4
EXN EX4 15 E5
EXS EX2 32 C2
HON EX14 6 C2
REXNE EX5 19 F2
REXSW EX6 43 E3
SID EX10 28 D5
SID EX10 38 C3
TOP/EXT EX3 43 F1
Station Yd EXN EX4 2 A2
Steel Cl HON EX14 5 F2
Steeple Dr EXS EX2 33 G4
Stepcote Hall EX EX1 2 B4
Stepcote Hl EXN EX4 * 2 A4
Steps Cl EX EX1 17 H4
Steven's Cross Cl SID EX10 31 G5
Stevens La SID EX10 38 C1
Stevenstone Rd EXM EX8 57 E5
Stewart Cl EXM EX8 57 F3
Stintway La SID EX10 38 A4
Stocker Rd EXN EX4 15 G4
Stoke Hl EXN EX4 16 B5
Stoke Hill Crs EXN EX4 16 B4
Stoke Lyne EXM EX8 56 D3
Stoke Meadow Cl EXN EX4 16 B3
Stoke Rd EXN EX4 15 F1
Stokes Md REXNE EX5 45 G3
Stoke Valley Rd EXN EX4 16 A2
Stoneborough La BUD EX9 59 G3
Stone Cl HON EX14 4 D4
Stone La EXM EX8 50 C4
Stoneyford Pk BUD EX9 59 G3
Stony La EXM EX8 50 D1
Stover Ct EXN EX4 2 E1
Stowford Ri SID EX10 30 B5
Strand TOP/EXT EX3 43 F2
The Strand EXM EX8 50 B4
EXM EX8 62 B1
REXSW EX6 55 E5
Strand Vw TOP/EXT EX3 43 F2
Stratford Av EXN EX4 17 F5
Strawberry Av EXS EX2 33 H3
Strawberry Hl EXM EX8 50 D4
Stream Ct EXS EX2 2 B6
Streamers Mdw HON EX14 5 E3
Streatham Dr EXN EX4 15 F5
Streatham Ri EXN EX4 15 F5
Stuart Rd EX EX1 3 K3
Sturges Rd EXM EX8 57 E4
Sullivan Rd EXS EX2 25 F3
Summer Cl EXM EX8 57 F4
EXN EX4 17 E5
Summerfield REXNE EX5 45 G2
SID EX10 30 D5
Summerland HON EX14 5 E3
Summerland St EXN EX4 2 E1
Summer La EXM EX8 56 B1
EXN EX4 17 E4
OTT EX11 13 H1
Summerway EXN EX4 17 E5
Sunhill Av TOP/EXT EX3 36 A5
Sunnyfield REXNE EX5 9 F3
Sunny Hl OTT EX11 13 E4
Sunnymoor Cl EX EX1 18 A4
Sunwine Pl EXM EX8 62 C1
Surbiton Crs EXN EX4 23 E4
Sussex Cl EXN EX4 22 D4
Swains Ct TOP/EXT EX3 * 43 E1
Swains Rd BUD EX9 59 G3
Swallow Dr EXS EX2 22 C5
Swallowfield Rd EXS EX2 34 D1
Swan Rd REXSW EX6 54 D4
Swan Yd EXN EX4 23 F3
HON EX14 5 E2
Sweetbrier La EX EX1 24 D2
Swiss Cl EXM EX8 56 C1
Sycamore Av DAW EX7 60 D5
Sycamore Cl EX EX1 25 E3
EXM EX8 57 F2
HON EX14 4 C5
REXNE EX5 9 G4
Sydney Pl EXS EX2 * 2 A6
Sydney Rd EXS EX2 23 F4
Sylvan Av EXN EX4 16 A4
Sylvan Cl EXM EX8 56 B2
Sylvania Dr EXN EX4 16 B3
Sylvan Rd EXN EX4 16 A4
Synagogue Pl EXN EX4 2 B3

T

Taddiford Rd EXN EX4 15 F5
Taddyforde Ct EXN EX4 * 15 F5
Taddyforde Est EXN EX4 * 15 F5
Taleford Cl OTT EX11 12 C1
Tamarisk Cl EXN EX4 17 E3
Tan La EXS EX2 23 G4
Tappers Cl TOP/EXT EX3 43 F1
Taps Cl REXSW EX6 42 B2
Tarbet Av EX EX1 24 C1
Taunton Cl EXS EX2 33 F1
Tavistock Rd EXN EX4 23 F1
Tedburn Rd EXN EX4 22 A3
Tedstone La EXM EX8 51 E4
Telegraph Hl REXSW EX6 46 C5
Telegraph La REXNE EX5 20 D2
Telford Rd EXN EX4 23 F1
Temple Rd EXS EX2 2 D5
Temple St SID EX10 38 D3
Tennyson Av EXS EX2 24 C5
Tennyson Wy EXM EX8 51 G5
Thackeray Rd EXN EX4 17 F5
Third Av EX EX1 3 J2
EXS EX2 35 G4
Thomas Cl EXM EX8 51 G5
Thomas La EXN EX4 * 15 F5
Thompson Rd EX EX1 24 D1
Thornberry Av EX EX1 25 E2
Thorn Cl EX EX1 25 E2
Thorne Farm Wy OTT EX11 12 C5
Thornfield Cl EXM EX8 56 B2
Thornpark Ri EX EX1 25 E2
Thornton Hl EXN EX4 15 H5
Thorpe Av EXM EX8 56 C1
Thorverton Rd EXS EX2 34 A3
Three Corner Pl EXS EX2 33 H3
Thurlow Rd EXN EX4 16 B5
Tidwell Cl BUD EX9 59 F2
Tidwell La BUD EX9 52 D4
Tidwell Rd BUD EX9 59 F2
Tintagel Cl EXN EX4 16 C3
Tip Hl OTT EX11 12 D5
Tithebarn Copse EX EX1 18 A5
Tithebarn La EX EX1 18 A5
Toadpit La OTT EX11 21 G2
Toby La REXNE EX5 45 H1
Tollards Rd EXS EX2 34 D2
Topsham Rd EXS EX2 2 E6
Tor Cl EXN EX4 16 D4
Toronto Rd EXN EX4 24 A1
Tottons Ct EXS EX2 33 F3
Towerfield TOP/EXT EX3 35 H4
Tower Rd HON EX14 5 H5
Tower St EXM EX8 62 B1
Tower Vw REXNE EX5 9 F5
Tower Wk EXS EX2 33 H3
Town End REXNE EX5 9 G3
Town Farm Cl HON EX14 4 D2
Townfield REXSW EX6 42 A2
Town Hl REXNE EX5 9 F3
Town La REXNE EX5 45 G3
Trafalgar Rd EXM EX8 50 C3
Traverses Cl EXM EX8 56 C3
Treasbeare La REXNE EX5 19 H3
Trefusis Pl EXM EX8 62 B2
Trefusis Ter EXM EX8 62 B2
Trefusis Wy BUD EX9 52 D3
Trelivan Cl EXM EX8 57 F1
Tremaine Cl HON EX14 5 F2
Trentbridge Sq EXS EX2 25 F4
Tresilian Gdns TOP/EXT EX3 43 F2
Tresillian Gdns EXN EX4 16 B5
Trews Weir Ct EXS EX2 2 E7
Trews Weir Reach EXS EX2 2 E7
Trinfield Av EXM EX8 56 C3
Trinity Rd EXM EX8 61 H1
Tristan Cl EXN EX4 16 D3
Trood La EXS EX2 34 A5
Trow Hl SID EX10 31 F5
Truro Dr EXM EX8 51 H5
EXN EX4 22 D1
Trusham Rd EXS EX2 33 H2
Tucker Ct HON EX14 5 E2
Tuckfield Cl EXS EX2 24 D4
Tudor Ct EXN EX4 2 A4
Tudor St EXN EX4 2 A4
Tugela Ter REXNE EX5 * 26 B5
Tully Gdns SID EX10 38 D1
Turkey La REXNE EX5 20 A2
Turner Av EXM EX8 56 D5
Turnpike HON EX14 5 F2
Tweed Cl HON EX14 5 E4
Twinaway La EXS EX2 32 B4
Twoacre Ct EXS EX2 33 F3
Two Bridges Rd SID EX10 31 E4
Two Stone La REXSW EX6 46 A1
Tyrrell Md SID EX10 38 D1

U

Underhill Crs EXM EX8 50 C5
Underhill Ter TOP/EXT EX3 43 F1
Under La SID EX10 31 H4
Unicorn St EXS EX2 25 G4
Union Rd EXN EX4 16 A5
Union St EXM EX8 62 B1
EXS EX2 23 F4
Upland Cha HON EX14 4 D5
Uplands Dr EXN EX4 16 C4
Upper Church St EXM EX8 62 B1
Upper Highfield SID EX10 38 C3
Upper Paul St EXN EX4 2 B2
Upper Stoneborough La BUD EX9 59 F3
Upper West Ter BUD EX9 59 F3
Upton Pyne Hl REXNE EX5 15 E1

V

Vale Rd EXM EX8 57 E5
Vales Rd BUD EX9 59 G3
Valley Park Cl EXN EX4 16 A3
Valley Rd EXN EX4 23 E1
REXNE EX5 27 E5
Valley Wy EXM EX8 57 F1
Vansittart Dr EXM EX8 56 D1
Varco Sq EXS EX2 25 F4
Vaughan Ri EX EX1 25 E2
Vaughan Rd EX EX1 25 E2
Veitch Gdns EXS EX2 33 G4
Velwell Rd EXN EX4 23 G1
Venn Ottery Rd SID EX10 28 B5
Venny Br EXN EX4 17 G4
Verney St EX EX1 2 E1
Vernon Rd EXM EX8 57 E2
Vestry Dr EXS EX2 33 G3
Vicarage Gdns EXS EX2 * 23 F4
Vicarage La EXN EX4 17 H3
Vicarage Rd BUD EX9 52 D3
REXSW EX6 61 E1
SID EX10 38 D4
Victor Cl EX EX1 24 D3
Victoria Cl REXSW EX6 54 A1
Victoria Park Rd EXS EX2 3 G5
Victoria Pl BUD EX9 59 F4
EXM EX8 62 B1
Victoria Rd EXM EX8 62 A1
EXN EX4 16 A5
SID EX10 38 C4
TOP/EXT EX3 43 F1
Victoria St EXN EX4 16 A5
Victoria Wy EXM EX8 62 A1
Victor La EX EX1 24 D3
Victor St EX EX1 24 D3
Vieux Cl BUD EX9 53 G2
Village Cl EXM EX8 57 G5
Vine Cl EXS EX2 2 E5
Vineycroft La SID EX10 31 H5
Vision Hill Rd BUD EX9 59 G2
Vuefield Hl EXS EX2 22 D5
Vyvyan Ct EX EX1 * 24 D3

W

Wade Cl EXM EX8 57 F4
Waggoners Wy EXN EX4 15 F5
Wallace Av EXN EX4 17 E5
Walls Cl EXM EX8 57 E2
Walnut Cl REXSW EX6 42 A2
Walnut Gv EXM EX8 56 D5
Walnut Rd EXS EX2 34 C1
HON EX14 4 C4
Walpole Cl EXN EX4 17 F4
Walsingham Pl EXS EX2 25 G4
Walsingham Rd EXS EX2 25 G4
Walton Rd EXS EX2 25 F3
Warborough Hl REXSW EX6 54 B2
Wardrew Rd EXN EX4 23 E4
Ware Ct HON EX14 4 C4
Waring Bowen Ct EXS EX2 * 34 C2
Warneford Gdns EXM EX8 57 F2
Warren Cl OTT EX11 21 F5
Warren Dr BUD EX9 59 G2
Warren La EXN EX4 2 D1
Warren Pk OTT EX11 21 F4
Warrens Md SID EX10 31 F5
Warwick Av EX EX1 25 F3
Warwick Cl HON EX14 7 E2
Warwick Rd EX EX1 25 F2
Warwick Wy EXN EX4 17 F5
Washbrook Vw OTT EX11 13 E4
Waterbeer St EXN EX4 * 2 B3
Water Ga EXS EX2 2 C5
Watering Ct BUD EX9 53 G2
Water La EXS EX2 2 C7
SID EX10 38 D3
Waterleat Av HON EX14 5 F3
Waterloo Rd EXS EX2 23 F5
Waterside EXS EX2 * 2 C6
Waterslade La REXNE EX5 19 E5
Watery La REXNE EX5 45 F2
Watson Pl EXS EX2 3 H7
Waverley Av EXN EX4 23 H1
Waverley Rd EXM EX8 56 B4
Waybrook Crs EXS EX2 33 H3
Waybrook La EXS EX2 33 F5
Wayland Av EXS EX2 3 F6
Wayside Crs EX EX1 25 E1
Wear Barton Rd EXS EX2 35 E3
Wear Cl EXS EX2 35 F4
Weatherill Rd HON EX14 5 E5
Webley Rd EXS EX2 23 E5
Weirfield Rd EXS EX2 2 D7
Welcome St EXS EX2 2 B7
Wellington Rd EXS EX2 23 F5
Well Oak Pk EXS EX2 24 C5
Wellpark Cl EXN EX4 23 E3
Wells Av HON EX14 6 D2
Well St EXN EX4 2 E1
REXSW EX6 55 E4
Wellswood Gdns EXN EX4 22 D3
Wendover Wy EXS EX2 35 E1
Wentworth Gdns EXN EX4 22 D4
Wesley Wy EXS EX2 33 G3
Wessex Cl TOP/EXT EX3 35 G5
Wessex Est EXN EX4 * 23 F1
West Av EXN EX4 15 H5
Westbourne Ter BUD EX9 59 E4
Westbridge Ct EXS EX2 34 A3
Westbrook Cl EXN EX4 17 E5
Westcombe EXS EX2 33 G3
Westcott Wy HON EX14 5 F2
West Down La EXM EX8 57 G5
Western Dr REXSW EX6 55 E4
Western Rd EXN EX4 23 F3
Western Wy EX EX1 2 B5
Westfield Cl BUD EX9 59 F3
Westfield Rd BUD EX9 59 F3
West Field Rd REXSW EX6 42 B3
West Garth Ct EXN EX4 * 15 E3
West Garth Rd EXN EX4 15 F3
West Grove Rd EXS EX2 2 E5
West Hl BUD EX9 59 E4
West Hill Ct BUD EX9 59 E4
West Hill Gdns BUD EX9 * 59 E4
West Hill La BUD EX9 59 E3
West Hill Rd OTT EX11 21 E5
Westminster Cl EXM EX8 57 E1
Westminster Rd EXN EX4 22 D2
Westown Rd EXS EX2 32 B2
West Park Rd SID EX10 38 C3
West St EX EX1 2 A4
West Ter BUD EX9 59 F3
EX EX1 3 K3
Westview Cl REXNE EX5 10 B2
West View Ter EXN EX4 * 2 A4
Westward Dr EXM EX8 56 C5
Westwood Hl REXSW EX6 60 D1
Westwood La REXSW EX6 22 A4
Weycroft Cl EX EX1 25 G2
Wheatley Cl EXN EX4 22 D3
Wheatsheaf Wy EXS EX2 33 F2
Whiddon La EXS EX2 32 A3
Whipton Barton Rd EX EX1 25 E1
Whipton La EX EX1 25 E2

Whipton Rd *EXN* EX4 ....16 D5
Whipton Village Rd *EXN* EX4 .....17 E5
Whitchurch Av *EXS* EX2 ....25 E4
Whitebeam Cl *EXN* EX4 ....17 E3
Whitebridges *HON* EX14 ....4 D4
White Farm La *OTT* EX11 ....21 F5
Whitehall La *TOP/EXT* EX3 ....35 H3
Whiteside Cl *EXS* EX2 ....25 F4
White St *TOP/EXT* EX3 ....43 F2
Whitethorn Cl *HON* EX14 ....5 E4
   SID EX10 ....30 B5
Whitethorn Pk *EXN* EX4 ....15 H2
Whiteway Dr *EX* EX1 ....24 D2
Whitman Cl *EXM* EX8 ....51 G5
Whitmore Wy *HON* EX14 ....4 C4
Whitycombe Wy *EXN* EX4 ....14 C5
Widecombe Wy *EXN* EX4 ....16 B3
Widgery Rd *EXN* EX4 ....16 D5
Wilcocks Rd *EXN* EX4 ....17 G4
Wilford Rd *EXS* EX2 ....25 E3
Willeys Av *EXS* EX2 ....2 A7
Willeys Ct *EXS* EX2 ....2 B7
Williams Av *EXS* EX2 ....2 A6
Willmott Cl *EXM* EX8 ....57 F3
Willoughby Cl *EXM* EX8 ....56 D1
Willow Av *EXM* EX8 ....24 D2
Willowbrook Av *EXN* EX4 ....17 F5
Willow Ct *EXS* EX2 ....24 D4
Willowdale Cl *HON* EX14 ....4 D2
The Willows *EXS* EX2 ....40 A2
Willow Wk *EXN* EX4 ....16 A5
   HON EX14 ....4 D4

Willow Wy *DAW* EX7 ....60 D5
   EXN EX4 ....17 F5
Willsdown Rd *EXS* EX2 ....33 G3
Willsland Cl *REXSW* EX6 ....54 A1
Wilton Wy *EX* EX1 ....25 C2
Wiltshire Cl *EXN* EX4 ....22 D4
Winchester Av *EXN* EX4 ....22 D1
Winchester Dr *EXM* EX8 ....51 H5
Windermere Cl *EXN* EX4 ....23 E3
Windjammer Ct *EXM* EX8 ....61 H1
Windmill La *OTT* EX11 ....21 F3
Windsor Cl *EXN* EX4 ....23 F1
Windsor Dr *DAW* EX7 ....60 B5
Windsor Md *SID* EX10 ....30 D4
Windsor Sq *EXM* EX8 ....56 B5
Winkleigh Cl *EXS* EX2 ....33 F1
Winneford La *HON* EX14 ....4 A2
Winslade Park Av *REXNE* EX5 .....36 B1
Winslade Rd *SID* EX10 ....38 C2
Winston Rd *EXM* EX8 ....57 F2
Winter's La *OTT* EX11 ....12 D5
Witcombe La *REXSW* EX6 ....54 A1
Witheby *SID* EX10 ....38 B5
The Withey *REXNE* EX5 ....10 B2
Withycombe Park Dr *EXM* EX8 ....57 F2
Withycombe Rd *EXM* EX8 ....56 B4
Withycombe Village Rd
   EXM EX8 ....56 C4
Wonford Rd *EXS* EX2 ....3 F5
Wonford St *EXS* EX2 ....24 D4
Woodah Rd *EXN* EX4 ....23 E3
Woodbine Ter *EXN* EX4 ....2 A1

Woodbury Rd *TOP/EXT* EX3 ....44 B1
Woodbury Vw *EXS* EX2 ....33 F1
Woodfield Cl *EXM* EX8 ....57 F2
Woodhill Vw *HON* EX14 ....4 D5
Woodland Rd *EX* EX1 ....25 G1
   REXNE EX5 ....9 G4
Woodlands *SID* EX10 ....38 C4
Woodlands Dr *EXM* EX8 ....56 C1
Woodlands Wy *REXNE* EX5 ....27 E5
Wood La *EXM* EX8 ....57 E3
Woodleigh Cl *EXN* EX4 ....15 F2
Woodmans Crs *HON* EX14 ....5 E3
Woodstock Rd *EXS* EX2 ....24 D3
Woodville Rd *EXM* EX8 ....56 B4
   EXS EX2 ....23 G5
Woodwater La *EXS* EX2 ....25 E4
Woolbrook Cl *SID* EX10 ....38 C2
Woolbrook Md *SID* EX10 ....38 B1
Woolbrook Mdw *SID* EX10 ....38 C1
Woolbrook Pk *SID* EX10 ....38 B1
Woolbrook Ri *SID* EX10 ....38 C1
Woolbrook Rd *SID* EX10 ....38 B1
Woolcombe La *SID* EX10 ....38 D3
Woolsery Av *EXN* EX4 ....17 E5
Woolsery Cl *EXN* EX4 ....17 E5
Woolsery Gv *EXN* EX4 ....16 D5
Woolway Av *REXSW* EX6 ....42 B2
Worcester Ms *EXN* EX4 * 22 D1
Wordsworth Cl *EXM* EX8 ....51 G5
Wotton La *EXM* EX8 ....51 E4
Wreford's Cl *EXN* EX4 ....15 F2
Wreford's Dr *EXN* EX4 ....15 F2

Wreford's La *EXN* EX4 ....15 F2
Wren Cl *HON* EX14 ....4 D4
Wrentham Est *EXN* EX4 * 16 A5
Wykes Rd *EX* EX1 ....24 C1
Wynards *EXS* EX2 * 2 D4
Wynards Cl *BUD* EX9 ....52 D3
Wynards Rd *BUD* EX9 ....52 D3
Wyndham Av *EX* EX1 ....3 J3
Wynford Rd *EXN* EX4 ....16 C4

Y

Yallop Wy *HON* EX14 ....4 D4
Yarde Cl *SID* EX10 ....38 D2
Yarde Hill Orch *SID* EX10 ....38 D1
Yardelands *SID* EX10 ....38 D1
Yardelands Cl *SID* EX10 ....38 D1
Yarde Md *SID* EX10 ....38 D1
Yeoford Wy *EXS* EX2 ....34 A3
Yettington Rd *BUD* EX9 ....52 C2
Yew Cl *HON* EX14 ....4 B4
Yew Tree Cl *EXM* EX8 ....56 D1
   EXN EX4 ....16 B4
Yonder Cl *OTT* EX11 ....13 E5
Yonder St *OTT* EX11 ....13 E5
York Crs *HON* EX14 ....4 D4
York Rd *EXN* EX4 ....2 D1
York St *SID* EX10 ....38 D5
York Ter *EXN* EX4 * 24 A1

Index - featured places

Abode Hotel *EX* EX1 ....2 C3
A La Ronde (NT) *EXM* EX8 ....56 B1
Alexandria Trading Estate *SID* EX10 ....38 C2
Alias Hotel Barcelona *EXS* EX2 .....2 D4
Allhallows Museum *HON* EX14 ......5 E2
All Saints CE Infant School *SID* EX10 ....38 D4
Alphington Combined School *EXS* EX2 ....33 G2
Alphington Sports Club *EXS* EX2 ....33 G2
Annexe London Hospital *EXN* EX4 ....15 H5
Ashton Business Centre *EXS* EX2 ....33 G1
Atkinson Unit *EXN* EX4 ....16 D5
Axehayes Farm Caravan Site *REXNE* EX5 ....27 G5
Barley Lane Special School *EXS* EX2 ....22 C4
Barnfield Theatre *EX* EX1 ....2 D3
The Beacon CE VA Primary School *EXM* EX8 ....62 A1
Bedford Hotel *SID* EX10 ....38 C5
Belmont Hotel *SID* EX10 ....38 C5
Best Western Gipsy Hill Country House Hotel *EX* EX1 ....18 A5
Bicton Mausoleum & Remains of Church *BUD* EX9 ....53 E1
Bicton Obelisk *BUD* EX9 ....53 E2
Bishops Court Industrial Estate *EXS* EX2 ....25 H5
Bonhay Business Centre *EXN* EX4 ....23 F3
Bowhill Primary School *EXN* EX4 ....23 E4
Bramble Hill Industrial Estate *HON* EX14 ....4 D2
Brixington Primary School *EXM* EX8 ....56 D2
Broadclyst Community Primary School *REXNE* EX5 ....9 F3
Buckerell Lodge Hotel *EXS* EX2 ....24 B5

Budleigh Salterton FC *BUD* EX9 ....59 E2
Budleigh Salterton Hospital *BUD* EX9 ....59 G3
Cadhay *OTT* EX11 ....12 B3
Cavendish Hotel *EXM* EX8 ....62 A1
City Industrial Estate *EXS* EX2 ....2 C7
Clifton Hill Sports Centre, Golf Range & Ski Slope *EX* EX1 ....3 G1
Clyst Heath Primary School *EXS* EX2 ....25 G5
Clyst Honiton School *REXNE* EX5 ....27 E1
Clyst St Mary Primary School *REXNE* EX5 ....26 B5
Clyst Vale Community College *REXNE* EX5 ....9 G5
Cockwood Primary School *REXSW* EX6 ....61 E1
Cofton Country Holidays *REXSW* EX6 ....60 C2
Coney Hill Cemetery *REXNE* EX5 ....10 B2
Countess Wear Combined School *EXS* EX2 ....35 E3
County Ground Stadium *EXS* EX2 ....23 F4
Cowley Bridge Road Business Park *EXN* EX4 ....15 E4
Crealy Adventure Park *REXNE* EX5 ....37 H1
Custom House *EXS* EX2 ....2 B5
Cygnet New Theatre *EX* EX1 ....2 C5
Darts Farm *TOP/EXT* EX3 ....43 H1
Dawlish Warren National Nature Reserve *DAW* EX7 ....61 F4
Devon Cliffs Holiday Park *EXM* EX8 ....63 H1
Devon & Exeter Squash Club *EXN* EX4 ....15 H5
Devon Hotel *EXS* EX2 ....34 A4
Devon Record Office *EXS* EX2 ....25 H2
Devoran Hotel *SID* EX10 ....38 D5
Dinan Way Trading Estate *EXM* EX8 ....57 G3

The Dolphin School *EXM* EX8 ....62 C1
Drakes Primary School *BUD* EX9 ....52 D3
Dunns Business Centre *EXM* EX8 ....33 H1
East Devon Golf Club *BUD* EX9 ....58 D4
Ellen Tinkham Special School *EX* EX1 ....25 H1
Emmanuel School *EXN* EX4 ....24 A1
Escot *OTT* EX11 ....6 A5
Exe Estuary RSPB Reserve *REXSW* EX6 ....42 D3
Exe Sailing Club *EXM* EX8 ....61 H1
The Exeter Academy *EXN* EX4 ....16 A4
Exeter Airport *REXNE* EX5 ....27 H1
Exeter Airport Business Park *REXNE* EX5 ....27 H1
Exeter Airport Industrial Estate *REXNE* EX5 ....27 H1
Exeter Business School *EXN* EX4 ....2 D2
Exeter Cathedral *EX* EX1 ....2 C3
Exeter Cathedral School *EX* EX1 ....2 C4
Exeter CC *EXN* EX4 ....15 H5
Exeter Cemetery *EX* EX1 ....3 K1
Exeter City FC *EXN* EX4 ....24 A1
Exeter College *EXN* EX4 ....2 A2
   EXS EX2 ....25 H4
   EXS EX2 ....33 H1
Exeter College (Episcopal Centre) *EXN* EX4 ....2 A3
Exeter College International Centre *EXN* EX4 ....23 F1
Exeter & Devon Crematorium *EXS* EX2 ....34 C1
Exeter Golf & Country Club *EXS* EX2 ....35 F3
The Exeter Nuffield Hospital *EXS* EX2 ....3 H6
Exeter Phoenix Arts Centre *EXN* EX4 ....2 B2
The Exeter Picture House *EXN* EX4 ....2 A4

Exeter Racecourse *REXSW* EX6 ....46 A5
Exeter RFC & Speedway *EXN* EX4 ....23 F4
Exeter Road Primary School *EXM* EX8 ....56 B5
Exeter Royal Academy for Deaf Education *EXS* EX2 ....2 E6
Exeter St Thomas CC *EXS* EX2 ....33 G1
Exeter School *EXS* EX2 ....3 H5
Exeter Technical College *EX* EX1 ....2 B4
Exminster Primary School *REXSW* EX6 ....42 A2
Exmouth Cemetery *EXM* EX8 ....57 G5
Exmouth Community College *EXM* EX8 ....56 C4
Exmouth CC *EXM* EX8 ....62 C2
Exmouth Hospital *EXM* EX8 ....56 C5
Exmouth Indoor Market *EXM* EX8 ....56 B5
Exmouth Leisure Centre *EXM* EX8 ....62 A1
Exmouth RFC *EXM* EX8 ....56 A5
Exmouth Town FC *EXM* EX8 ....56 B4
Express by Holiday Inn *EX* EX1 ....25 H2
Exwick Heights Primary School *EXN* EX4 ....22 D1
Fairlynch Museum *BUD* EX9 ....59 G4
Feniton CE Primary School *HON* EX14 ....6 D2
Finnimore Industrial Estate *OTT* EX11 ....12 C5
The Globe Hotel *TOP/EXT* EX3 ....43 F2
Great Western Business Park *EXN* EX4 ....4 B4
Great Western Hotel *EXN* EX4 ....23 F1
Harlequins Shopping Centre *EXN* EX4 ....2 B2
Haven Banks Sailing & Canoeing Club *EXS* EX2 ....2 C6
Hayes Barton (Home of Sir Walter Raleigh) *BUD* EX9 ....52 A2
Heavitree Health Centre *EX* EX1 ....3 K3

Hill Barton Business Park
REXNE EX5 ....**37** G1
HM Prison Exeter
EXN EX4 ....**2** B1
Honeylands Hospital for
Children *EXN* EX4 ....**17** E5
Honiton Business Park
HON EX14 ....**4** D2
Honiton Community College
HON EX14 ....**5** E2
Honiton Golf Club
HON EX14 ....**5** G5
Honiton Hospital
HON EX14 ....**5** E3
Honiton Primary School
HON EX14 ....**5** E1
Honiton Sports Centre
HON EX14 ....**4** D2
Hope House Montessori School
TOP/EXT EX5 ....**43** F2
Hunters Moon Hotel
SID EX10 ....**38** D3
Hylton Pre Preparatory School
EXS EX2 ....**3** D5
Ide Primary School
EXS EX2 ....**32** D2
Innkeeper's Lodge
TOP/EXT EX5 ....**43** H1
Isca College of Media Arts
EXS EX2 ....**34** B1
Kenn CE Primary School
REXSW EX6 ....**40** D5
Kennford International
Caravan Park
REXSW EX6 ....**46** C1
Kenton Primary School
REXSW EX6 ....**54** A1
Kestrel Business Park
EXS EX2 ....**35** G2
Kingsgate Business Centre
HON EX14 ....**4** C4
The Kings School
OTT EX11 ....**12** B5
Kingswood Hotel
SID EX10 ....**38** C5
Lady Seawards CE Primary
School
TOP/EXT EX5 ....**36** D5
Ladysmith Infant School
EX EX1 ....**3** H1
Ladysmith Junior School
EX EX1 ....**3** H1
Langdon Hospital
DAW EX7 ....**60** B4
Little Bridge Business Park
REXNE EX5 ....**37** E2
Littleham CE Primary School
EXM EX8 ....**57** G5
Littletown Primary School
HON EX14 ....**5** E4
Liverton Business Park
EXM EX8 ....**57** G3
Lodge Trading Estate
REXNE EX5 ....**19** F2
Longbrook Complementary
Health Centre
EXN EX4 ....**2** D1
Lympstone CE Primary School
EXM EX8 ....**50** C4
Maer Local Nature Reserve
EXM EX8 ....**63** E3
Magdalen Court School
EXS EX2 ....**3** G5
Manor Hotel
EXM EX8 ....**62** B1
Manor House School
HON EX14 ....**5** H3
Manstree
EXS EX2 ....**40** A1
Marker's Cottage (NT)
REXNE EX5 ....**9** G3
Marpool Primary School
EXM EX8 ....**56** D4
Marsh Barton Trading Estate
EXS EX2 ....**33** H2
The Maynard School
EX EX1 ....**3** F3
Meadow House Clinic
EXN EX4 ....**23** G1
Megabowl
EXS EX2 ....**2** C6
Mercure Southgate Hotel
EX EX1 ....**2** C4
Meteorological Office
EX EX1 ....**25** G1
Mill Water Special School
HON EX14 ....**5** E4
Mol's Coffee House
EX EX1 ....**2** C3

Montgomery Combined School
EXN EX4 ....**23** E3
Mount Pleasant Health Centre
EXN EX4 ....**16** B5
Mount Pleasant Hotel
SID EX10 ....**38** D4
The New School
REXSW EX6 ....**42** A2
Newton Poppleford Primary
School *SID* EX10 ....**28** D5
Newtown First School
EX EX1 ....**3** F2
Northcott Theatre
EXN EX4 ....**15** G4
Northernhay Gate
EXN EX4 ....**2** B2
Nutwell Court
EXM EX8 ....**50** B2
Odeon Cinema
EX EX1 ....**2** E1
The Old Gasworks
REXSW EX6 ....**54** C1
Old Tudor House
EXN EX4 ....**23** F3
Otterton Mill
BUD EX9 ....**53** F2
Otterton Primary School
BUD EX9 ....**53** G2
Ottery St Mary Primary
School
OTT EX11 ....**13** E5
Park Five Business Centre
EXS EX2 ....**25** H4
Peppermint Park
DAW EX7 ....**61** E5
Pinbrook Industrial Estate
EXN EX4 ....**17** G4
Pinhoe CE Combined School
EXN EX4 ....**17** H4
Pooh Cottage Holiday Park
BUD EX9 ....**58** C1
Post Graduate Medical School
EXS EX2 ....**3** J5
Pound Lane Trading Estate
EXM EX8 ....**56** D3
Powderham Castle
REXSW EX6 ....**49** F5
Prattshayes Farm National
Trust Campsite
EXM EX8 ....**63** F1
Princesshay Shopping Centre
EX EX1 ....**2** C3
Pyramids Swimming & Leisure
Centre *EX* EX1 ....**2** E2
Quay House Visitor Centre
EXS EX2 ....**2** B5
Queens Court Hotel
EXN EX4 ....**2** A1
Radway Cinema
SID EX10 ....**38** C4
Redhills Combined School
EXN EX4 ....**23** E3
Red House Hotel
EXN EX4 ....**16** D5
River Exe Country Park
EXS EX2 ....**34** C3
Riverside Leisure Centre
EXN EX4 ....**2** A6
Riviera Hotel
SID EX10 ....**38** D5
Rolle Clinic
EXM EX8 ....**62** B1
Rougemont Castle
EXN EX4 ....**2** C1
Royal Albert Memorial Museum
EXN EX4 ....**2** B2
Royal Beacon Hotel
EXM EX8 ....**62** B1
Royal Devon & Exeter Hospital
(Heavitree) *EX* EX1 ....**3** C3
Royal Devon & Exeter Hospital
(Wonford)
EXS EX2 ....**3** J6
Royal Glen Hotel
SID EX10 ....**38** C5
The Royal York & Faulkner
Hotel
SID EX10 ....**38** D5
St Davids Primary School
EXN EX4 ....**2** A2
St Georges Hall & Market
EXN EX4 ....**2** B3
St James School
EXN EX4 ....**17** E4
St James Sports Centre
EXN EX4 ....**17** E4
St Johns Caravan & Camping
Park
EXM EX8 ....**57** G1

St Johns School
SID EX10 ....**38** B3
St Josephs Catholic Primary
School
EXM EX8 ....**56** C5
St Leonards Primary School
EXS EX2 ....**2** E6
St Loyes Foundation
EXS EX2 ....**34** C1
St Loyes School of Occupational
Therapy
EXS EX2 ....**34** C1
St Lukes Science & Sports
College
EX EX1 ....**17** G5
St Margarets School
EXS EX2 ....**3** H4
St Michaels VA Primary School
EXN EX4 ....**3** K3
St Nicholas CE Junior School
SID EX10 ....**38** C1
St Nicholas RC Combined
School *EXS* EX2 ....**2** E6
St Olaves Hotel
EXN EX4 ....**2** A3
St Peters CE Aided School
EXS EX2 ....**25** F3
St Peters CE Primary School
BUD EX9 ....**59** E2
St Peters School
EXM EX8 ....**51** E3
St Sidwells CE Primary School
EXN EX4 ....**23** H1
St Thomas Cemetery
EXS EX2 ....**23** E2
St Thomas Health Centre
EXS EX2 ....**23** E4
St Thomas Primary School
EXS EX2 ....**23** F4
St Thomas Shopping Centre
EXS EX2 ....**23** F3
St Wilfrids School
EXS EX2 ....**23** F2
Sidbury CE Primary School
SID EX10 ....**31** G1
Sidmouth Cemetery
SID EX10 ....**38** D2
Sidmouth College
SID EX10 ....**39** E1
Sidmouth Golf Club
SID EX10 ....**38** A5
Sidmouth Hospital
SID EX10 ....**38** C4
Sidmouth Infant School
SID EX10 ....**38** D1
Southbrook School
EXS EX2 ....**34** D1
Sowton Industrial Estate
EXS EX2 ....**25** H3
Starcross Primary School
REXSW EX6 ....**54** D4
Starcross Yacht Club
REXSW EX6 ....**49** H4
Stoke Hill Infant School
EXN EX4 ....**16** B4
Stoke Hill Junior School
EXN EX4 ....**16** B4
Stone Lane Retail Park
EXS EX2 ....**23** G5
Summerway Middle School
EXN EX4 ....**17** F5
Thistle Hotel
EX EX1 ....**2** B2
Thorntree Business Units
EXS EX2 ....**57** G3
Tipton St John Primary School
SID EX10 ....**28** D1
Topsham Cemetery
TOP/EXT EX3 ....**36** A5
Topsham Museum
TOP/EXT EX3 ....**43** F2
Topsham RFC
TOP/EXT EX3 ....**35** H5
Topsham Sailing Club
TOP/EXT EX3 ....**43** E1
The Topsham School
TOP/EXT EX3 ....**43** E1
Topsham Town AFC
TOP/EXT EX3 ....**35** H5
Tor College of Nursing
EXS EX2 ....**3** J4
Travelodge
EXS EX2 ....**26** A4
Tucker's Hall
EX EX1 ....**2** A4
Tumbling Weir Hotel
OTT EX11 ....**12** C5
University of Exeter
EXN EX4 ....**2** E1

EXS EX2 ....**3** G5
University of Exeter
(Duryard Halls)
EXN EX4 ....**15** F3
University of Exeter
(St Luke's Campus)
EX EX1 ....**3** F3
University of Exeter
(Streatham Campus)
EXN EX4 ....**15** G5
University of Plymouth
(Exeter Campus)
EXS EX2 ....**24** B5
University of Plymouth
(Exmouth Campus)
EXM EX8 ....**62** C2
Victoria Hotel
SID EX10 ....**38** C5
Victoria Park Tennis & Bridge
Club
EXS EX2 ....**3** C5
Vranch House School
EXN EX4 ....**25** H1
Vue Cinema
EX EX1 ....**2** E2
Walter Daw First School
EXS EX2 ....**25** E4
Warren Golf Club
DAW EX7 ....**61** E5
Webbers Farm Caravan
& Camping Park
REXNE EX5 ....**45** H3
Westcliff Hotel
SID EX10 ....**38** C5
West Exe Technology College
EXS EX2 ....**33** F1
West Hill Primary School
OTT EX11 ....**21** F4
West of England School &
College
EXS EX2 ....**35** E2
Westpoint (Devon County
Showground)
REXNE EX5 ....**26** D5
Whimple Primary School
REXNE EX5 ....**10** A2
Whipton Barton First School
EXN EX4 ....**17** E5
Whipton Barton Junior School
EXN EX4 ....**25** E1
Whipton Hospital
EX EX1 ....**25** F1
Willeys Sports Club
EXS EX2 ....**2** C7
Willowbrook School
EXN EX4 ....**17** E4
Withycombe Raleigh CE
Primary School
EXM EX8 ....**56** D3
Withycombe RFC
EXM EX8 ....**56** C3
Wonford House Hospital
EXS EX2 ....**3** K7
Wonford Sports Centre
EXS EX2 ....**24** D5
Woodbury Cemetery
REXNE EX5 ....**45** G3
Woodbury CE Primary School
REXNE EX5 ....**45** G3
The Woodlands Hotel
SID EX10 ....**38** C4
Wrentham Business Centre
EXN EX4 ....**16** A5
Wynstream Primary School
EXS EX2 ....**24** C5

Schools address data provided by Education Direct.

Petrol station information supplied by Johnsons

Garden Centre Association  Britains best garden centres

Wyevale Garden Centres

The statement on the front cover of this atlas is sourced, selected and quoted from a reader comment and feedback form received in 2004

Speed camera locations

Speed camera locations provided in association with RoadPilot Ltd

RoadPilot

RoadPilot is the developer of one of the largest and most accurate databases of speed camera locations in the UK and Europe. It has provided the speed camera information in this atlas. RoadPilot is the UK's pioneer and market leader in GPS (Global Positioning System) road safety technologies.

microGo (pictured right) is RoadPilot's latest in-car speed camera location system. It improves road safety by alerting you to the location of accident black spots.

fixed and mobile camera sites. RoadPilot's microGo does not jam police lasers and is therefore completely legal.

RoadPilot's database of fixed camera locations has been compiled with the full co-operation of regional police forces and the Safety Camera Partnerships.

For more information on RoadPilot's GPS road safety products, please visit **www.roadpilot.com** or telephone 0870 240 1701

GPS Antenna
microGo is directional, it only alerts you to cameras on your side of the road

Visual Countdown
To camera location

Your Speed
The speed you are travelling when approaching camera

Camera Types Located
Gatso, Specs, Truvelo, TSS/DSS, Traffipax, mobile camera sites, accident black spots, congestion charges, tolls

Voice Warnings
Only if you are exceeding the speed limit at the camera

ALARM MODE

Plug and Go
Easy to move from vehicle to vehicle

64 Colour Options
To match vehicle's illumination

Speed Limit at Camera
Screen turns red as additional visual alert

Single Button Operation
For easy access to speed display, camera warning, rescue me location, trip computer, congestion charge, max speed alarm, date and time

SPEED READING